THE ART OF PICTURE RESEARCH

THE
ART OF PICTURE RESEARCH

A Guide to Current Practice, Procedure,
Techniques and Resources

HILARY EVANS

DAVID & CHARLES

NEWTON ABBOT   LONDON   NORTH POMFRET (Vt)

This book is dedicated to Judith Byrne, Janet Grillet, Susan Pinkus and Mari Zipes, who have done so much to turn the British Picture Researcher into a professional.

I am also grateful to a great many people, picture researchers and others, who have allowed me to draw upon their knowledge and experience. In particular I would like to thank: Jane Ades, Edward Birch, Julia Brown, Anne-Marie Ehrlich, Robert Harding, Ann Horton, and Anne Williams.

British Library Cataloguing in Publication Data

Evans, Hilary
   The art of picture research.
   1. Pictures
   I. Title
   001.55'35   Z692.P5

  ISBN 0–7153–7763–9

© Hilary Evans 1979

Photoset and printed in Great Britain
by Redwood Burn Limited, Trowbridge & Esher
for David & Charles (Publishers) Limited
Brunel House Newton Abbot Devon

Published in the United States of America
by David & Charles Inc
North Pomfret Vermont 05053 USA

Contents

Preface

If you attend a concert at the Festival Hall, there may be a portrait of
Mozart in the programme: someone had to get that portrait from
somewhere. If you buy a box of chocolates with a picture of a fluffy
kitten on it, someone had to find that picture of a fluffy kitten. If you
read a magazine article about housing which contrasts an engraving
of Victorian slums with a photo of a modern housing estate, someone
had to obtain the engraving from one source, the photo from another,
and bring the two together. Every picture you ever see reproduced
was obtained by somebody from somewhere: the process of obtaining
that picture, however simple or complex, is picture research.

Reduced to basics, picture research sounds simple enough:

- Establish what pictures are required
- Discover where to find them
- Locate, select, and make arrangements to obtain them

At its simplest, there is little more to the job than that. But it is rarely
so simple: each of those stages can involve infinite complications.
Different kinds of picture must be found to meet different needs;
every user of pictures has his own way of working; pictures are
available in countless different forms; the sources from which they
are obtained vary in size and scope, in the fees they charge and the
services they offer, in the conditions they impose and the procedure
they require you to adopt.

So the picture researcher's task is an infinite one: she* will be continually adding to her store of experience till the day she retires. This
book cannot contain the whole of even one researcher's lifetime of
experience, but it seeks to show the main varieties of procedure that
you may encounter, and to explain some of the niceties of the business. At
the same time it examines the reasons for practices which may on the

---

* For convenience's sake I have opted to refer to the researcher as 'she' and the client who
commissions her as 'he', to avoid writing 'he or she' every time. No sexist discrimination is
intended. However, membership of SPREd (see 1.07) is 90 per cent female.

surface seem arbitrary and even idiosyncratic. It will have served its purpose if it can clear up some of the misunderstandings which frequently occur, and if, by encouraging researchers to understand their work more fully it can help them do it more fruitfully and enjoyably.

At the same time, this book is intended not only for the picture researcher herself, but also for those who employ her and use her services, that they may appreciate the scope and complexity of her task; and for those who provide her with the pictures she seeks, that they may appreciate her problems, help her to surmount them, and, in so doing, make their own job easier.

PART ONE

THE PICTURE RESEARCHER

1.01 A New Profession

Until recently it was rare for the name of a picture researcher to appear among the list of credits for those responsible for producing a book, a periodical or a television programme. Today this is becoming more and more customary, a recognition that the picture researcher plays a vital and often very creative role.

A picture researcher may be employed by an advertising agency, an audio-visual producer, a book publisher, an exhibition designer, a filmstrip producer, a museum, a packaging firm, a periodical publisher, a television company, a theatre designer—or by many other types of business. The emphasis in this book is on book production, partly because the majority of picture researchers are concerned with books and partly because picture research for books is picture research at its most complex. Though you work, or plan to work, in some other field, you will find most of what follows relevant.

The professional picture researcher is a relatively recent arrival on the scene. Even a decade ago most picture research was carried out by people whose primary functions were as editors, designers, or even publishers' assistants. They did their picture research as well as they could, learning from more experienced colleagues who could tell them where to go and how to proceed. But it was all rather haphazard, and the quality of the finished work depended entirely on the calibre of the individual researcher.

Well, that is still true, but today's researcher is more likely to be aware of her responsibilities and, if she is lucky, those who employ her will be aware of them too. If she is conscientious she will have studied to acquire the skill and proficiency required; she may even have been lucky enough to receive some formal training, although even today this is not readily available. The formation of SPREd in Britain, and similar organisations in the United States and France, is a sign that picture research is at last recognised as a profession in its own right. This means that those who venture to practise it must take it seriously and ensure that they possess the necessary skills and knowledge.

What, then, does the picture researcher's job entail? First, the recognition that pictures exist in many different forms, from cave paintings to cinema stills, from old master paintings to holiday snaps, and that all these and countless others (see section 4.01) have their value to the researcher.

Second, the fact that these pictures can be found in an astonishing variety of places, from State archives to private collections, from streamlined commercial phototeques to the leatherbound archives of professional institutions. The researcher must learn to cast her net widely if she is not to miss some of the most rewarding material.

These two aspects form the subject matter of Part Two of this guide.

Finding the material is only the first stage, however. Next comes the business of obtaining it—with all the complexities of copyright, permissions, fees and rights, plus the routine paperwork of keeping track of which pictures came from where, and when, and how long they can be kept, etc. The multifarious aspects of procedure on a research assignment are covered in Part Three.

Over and above knowing her way around the world of pictures, the researcher must know more than a little about pictures themselves. A picture which is suitable for one purpose is not right for another. An illustration suitable for a popular history may not be appropriate in a scholarly treatise; the low-grade paper used for newspapers does not reproduce pictures to the same high quality as a glossy magazine. And, even when a suitable picture has been found, there are factors such as cost to be taken into account. Part Four seeks to cover, as simply as possible, the intricacies of picture selection.

Clearly, so wide-ranging a task calls for considerable expertise, and this situation alone would inevitably have in time created a breed of specialists. But the process has been accelerated by two additional factors. The first is the growth of the heavily illustrated book, made possible by the technological advances of recent decades. One has only to visit any bookstore—even a railway bookstall—to see the proliferation of handsome, well produced illustrated books on a staggering range of subjects, books of a type which simply didn't exist twenty or thirty years ago. Though a few of these qualify for the derogatory term of 'coffee-table books', the great majority are well made and useful. In this dazzling revolution the picture researcher has necessarily played a vital rôle, and perhaps no other single factor has emphasised more strongly her value to her employer.

At the same time, costs of books have gone up, reflecting the cost of printing, the cost of paper, the cost of distribution. Each of these handsome books in the bookstores is the result of a very substantial financial investment by the publisher; and, though he may do his best to make sure of his market before embarking on the venture, in the end publishing remains largely what it has always been, a gamble. So the publisher protects himself as best he can; and one of his protections is to make sure that the pictures which play so important a part in his venture are selected and obtained as efficiently as possible. Once again, the researcher has come to play a central rôle.

The consequence is that, among the major publishers at any rate, the picture researcher's job is now taken very seriously indeed, and the researcher herself is accorded the status she deserves. The corollary is, of course, that she herself must learn to take her job very seriously, and ensure that she is fully qualified to take on such responsibility.

So, before we go into the complexities of the researcher's work, let us in Part One look at what opportunities are open to her, and what resources exist to help her equip herself to make the most of those opportunities.

1.02 Qualifications and Training

As yet there are no formal qualifications for the picture researcher. Perhaps there never will be, and maybe that's just as well. For the fact is that almost any kind of training or experience can be of value: at the same time, paradoxically, it is equally a fact that no training or experience can effectively replace the 'nose' of a researcher endowed with real flair.

But flair, while easy to recognise, is hard to evaluate. Most employers prefer more solid yardsticks, at least as a starting point. Many will expect aspiring researchers to come to them, if not with a university degree, at least with solid educational qualifications of some kind, not so much for the knowledge thus acquired as for the discipline the student will have learnt while acquiring that knowledge. The one asset a picture researcher just cannot manage without is quite simply the ability to carry out research; a university degree is— or should be—an indication that the student has learned to handle research tools. At the same time it is no guarantee of capability: it is equally a fact that many who have no educational qualifications *do* possess the appropriate talents. However, you must be prepared to meet employers who, unwilling to gamble on their own intuitions, look for objective evaluations of your potential performance.

Some subjects will of course be more useful than others. A training in art history is of obvious benefit, though it is probable that this is best acquired as a postgraduate, at some such institution as the *Courtauld Institute* (see 1.07). The knowledge acquired on such a course will certainly be of value, though once the researcher goes to work she will find she has to temper her academic learning with more practical experience: when assessing an illustration for reproduction there are many other criteria besides the aesthetic. She will learn that an anonymous artist's view of Brighton 'may be preferable to a Turner, despite crude drawing and faulty perspective, simply because it conveys more information; that a picture which reproduces well may be preferable to a fine painting which after printing is a vague blotch; that a fine picture from an expensive source may have to be rejected in favour of a poorer one from a cheaper source, simply on financial grounds.

In other words, picture research is concerned very much with practicalities: any formal knowledge you have acquired may be used only marginally. More important is the overall attitude your learning has engendered, the sense of method. Your employers won't expect you to know the name of Edward III's wife, but they'll expect you to know how to find out. A knowledge, and even more importantly a *sense* of history are indispensable for most fields of research, even when the subject itself is not a historical one, for many illustrations can be fully evaluated only in a historical context. A book on stained glass or whaling will be the better if those concerned have a historical grasp of the subject.

Knowing the business

Research is only part of the researcher's work: you must also have a clear understanding of what you are researching *for*. No employer will expect a newcomer to the profession to know very much about the business until she's acquired some experience: most such knowledge will come as a side-result of doing the actual work. But it would be a serious mistake to go into the business without having some notion of what it's all about.

For example, some knowledge of printing and reproduction is sure to be valuable, and it will get you off to a good start if you have given yourself a slight grounding in these subjects. There are many good books (see 1.08) which will serve as an introduction: these can be supplemented by visits to such institutions as the *Victoria & Albert Museum*, where informative exhibits present the processes in tangible form. If you can arrange to visit a printing works, do so: you will find it dismayingly complicated and confusing, but the experience will give you some idea of the immense complexity of the process of picture-using of which you, as the researcher, represent one of the early stages.

Courses in some of these subjects have been arranged for certain categories of trainee, but they are generally limited to membership of organisations such as the *Publishers Association* or the *Art Libraries Society* (see 1.07). In due course it may be hoped that SPREd (1.07) will make such training opportunities more readily available. Once you have started work, you may be able to persuade your employer to enrol you in one of these courses, but your chances of getting onto one before you are employed are very slight. Nor, as yet, are there any evening classes in picture research, though this is something we shall surely see before very long.

Learning about publishing

If, like the majority of picture researchers, you expect to be working mainly for book or periodical publishers, you should try to acquire a knowledge of books and the book trade. You should learn how books are made, and how pictures are prepared for reproduction; you should also learn something about the book trade, about the kinds of book that are published, and why they are the way they are. Aspects of these matters are touched on at various points in this guide, but nothing replaces personal experience. Talk to anybody who knows anything about books, take a temporary job in a bookshop, learn to look at them not only as vehicles of communication but also as manufactured articles, representing the combined efforts of many specialist skills of which yours is just one.

The best place to see books is at the various Book Fairs. Easily the most important is the Frankfurt Book Fair, held in Germany every autumn. To visit this Fair is an experience to which every Picture Researcher should treat herself (or persuade her employer to treat her) at least once in her career, for nowhere else will she come up against the realities of the publishing world in so dramatic a manner, seeing what sorts of books are produced by what people and in what form. There are also Book Fairs in Nice, Bologna, Montreal and elsewhere, and a smallish but growing one in London just before the Frankfurt Fair, which should not be missed by British researchers because it provides you with an opportunity to see what some of Britain's smaller publishers are doing.

Other fields

It is less easy to prepare for a research career in one of the non-publishing fields, such as television or exhibition design, for here the work is more specifically geared to the medium. However, the very fact that you have opted for this particular direction suggests that you have some previous knowledge of it: you will clearly need to inform yourself of its special requirements. Finding the illustrations is much the same whatever you're finding them for, but the criteria you apply won't necessarily be the same—the picture that looks good on the printed page won't necessarily be so effective on an exhibition panel four metres wide. The techniques of television enable pictures to be given an extra dimension—the camera can pan across a very detailed picture, highlighting a piece of it at a time, or zoom in on a specific detail of a larger picture. It's a healthy exercise, whenever you watch television or visit an exhibition, to try to imagine what were the criteria applied by the researcher who found the pictures.

Besides standing you in good stead when you start your career, this kind of familiarity with your subject will pay off even at your interviews. You will be able to give more intelligent answers to questions, and your acquaintance with some of the problems will indicate that you've taken the trouble to learn a little about the business—an encouraging character indication!

Qualification check-list

To sum up then, ideally, when you offer yourself as a picture researcher you should be able to offer your employer some such qualifications as these:

- A university degree (subject not crucial), preferably followed by a postgraduate course in art history; or educational qualifications of some kind, preferably in art/history/art history; plus, if possible, attendance at a training course
- Some knowledge, appropriate to the field you've chosen, of:
  book production
  magazine production
  television production
  exhibition techniques
  printing processes
  reproduction techniques
  the book trade
  illustration techniques
  basic principles of photography
- Familiarity with basic research tools—works of reference, library systems, cataloguing methods
- You should, in addition, be neat and orderly by temperament—at any rate in your business life. You should be able to write a simple, polite, informative letter. You should be able to type.

Above, behind the scenes at the
British Museum in 1875: it's all
there, if you can find it . . .

Below left, a rare portrait:
Dr Guillotin, depicted by the
printmaker four years before the
fall of the Bastille

Just look at him! there he stands
With his nasty hair and hands.
See! the horrid blood drops drip
From each dirty finger tip;
And the sloven, I declare,
Never once has combed his hair;
Piecrust never could be brittler
Than the word of Adolf Hitler.

Which is the real Adolf Hitler?

As an indication of the sort of knowledge you would be well-advised to possess from the start, here are some basic questions to which you should be able to offer at least some kind of intelligent answer:

● Which of two otherwise equally suitable illustrations would you choose for reproduction in a daily newspaper—a drawing or a photograph? Why?
● Why is it more expensive to print colour pictures than black and white?
● Why do some books have the illustrations on the same pages as the text while others have them on separate pages?
● A magazine like *New Society* carries advertisements, a publication like *Tree of Knowledge* doesn't. Why the difference?
● An author recently told his publisher he could provide all the illustrations needed for his book, and produced a heap of photos he had personally copied from the *National Geographic Magazine*. Why was his editor left speechless?
● Your employer wants to reproduce the famous Dürer drawing of praying hands. How will you help him do so?

1.03 Rewards and Drawbacks

Every job offers two kinds of reward: the tangible (money or the equivalent) and the intangible (job satisfaction). Picture research offers a fair balance of the two. There are aspects of picture research which can be tedious and frustrating—this guide makes no attempt to hide the fact!—but, at the same time, few jobs offer as much scope for individual initiative and personal responsibility. Ultimately here, as everywhere, it's a question of temperament.

First, what about the tangible rewards? Salaries vary considerably in this unorganised profession, though we can expect to see a greater degree of uniformity emerging very rapidly over the next few years, thanks to the formation of SPREd and other organisations. In the summer of 1979, starting salaries were in the £2,750–£3,750 range, the higher figure going to a novice who could offer a degree or other higher qualifications. After four years, a staff researcher could expect to have passed the £4,000 mark. Much depends on the degree of responsibility she is asked—and prepared—to shoulder.

Freelance rates are very flexible, and affected by many factors (see 3.05). By and large, a capable freelance researcher can expect to earn between £4,000 and £5,000—but to earn that she is going to have to work herself hard and organise herself ruthlessly.

The intangibles

Working as a freelance to whom a complete assignment has been handed over is very different from working as a member of a team on an encyclopedia, where most of the research work consists of letters and 'phone calls. So the intangibles are apt to vary even more than the tangible rewards. Not all the following will be encountered on any one job, but here are some of the attractions of the picture researcher's life.

Working with pictures

If you don't find that a reward in itself, you shouldn't be in the business!

Working with congenial and interesting people

By and large, publishing, documentary television and exhibition design are staffed by intelligent, creative people who are stimulating to work with. There are bores and nasties in every business, but perhaps fewer here than in most.

Visiting interesting places

You won't be visiting stately homes to ask the Duke if you can photograph his ancestral home every day of the week, but it happens. So do foreign trips. But even nearer home, visiting obscure collections, briefing photographers, meeting eccentric owners, finding your way through the labyrinths of national archives, is often fascinating and rarely totally boring.

The chance to be out and about

This varies a lot, and could well govern your choice of employers, according to whether you prefer the stability of established routine or the stimulus of something different every day.

A considerable degree of personal responsibility

This also varies a lot, of course, and tends to increase as you gain experience and your employer's respect. After a while you will find yourself in a position to make a positive creative contribution to the work, but this will in turn be a responsibility, knowing that the success of a costly project depends in some part on your ability.

Job satisfaction

Every assignment is, ultimately, a treasure hunt: when you set out, you may not know exactly what you are looking for, or, if you do, what your chances are of finding it. The excitement of finding out is at the heart of the researcher's job.

Drawbacks

All these benefits are obtained at a price. Largely, it's a matter of hard work and application; but there are also some character traits which will stand you in good stead. To obtain some pictures from some sources presents no problem: looking for a portrait of Mary Queen of Scots, say, you can just make an appointment to visit the Mansell Collection, or simply 'phone them, and that's just about all there is to it apart from the paperwork. But for every straightforward assignment there's at least one dodgy one. There are the tough Fleet Street press agencies, where you will have to learn to hold your own with a toughness to match theirs; and there are the dedicated collectors who don't really want you to have their material, who will demand all your diplomacy to obtain what you want. You will have to learn to alter your attitude depending on the people you're talking to: to adapt to the differing requirements of, say, the British Museum Print Room or the Royal Aeronautical Society or the Duke of Bedford or the little old lady in Bournemouth who has that unique collection of straw dollies . . .

And you will need other character traits to cope with the people back in the office. You will have to learn to put up with disappointment—when projects are cancelled, when layout demands mean that a picture you spent hours or even days trying to find has to be omitted, when an author tells you that the picture you're so proud to have found isn't what he had in mind. . . . Besides your own personal disappointment, you will have the wretched job of going back to your source and telling them in turn the bad news, and you will have to accept that, however innocent and well intentioned, you, as the representative of your company, will be blamed for it.

1.04 Career Opportunities (1) Staff

Firms who employ picture researchers may do so in three ways:

- Full-time picture researchers, designated as such
- As one of several functions carried out by people with such job designations as Art Editor, Art Buyer, Editorial Assistant, and so on
- Freelance researchers employed on either a retainer or an assignment basis.

As more books tend to be generously illustrated, more and more publishers are employing full-time picture researchers, since this is clearly the most efficient way of securing the services of an experienced person who will also have the advantage of being familiar with that company's procedure and practice. But sometimes the volume of work doesn't justify this, and so picture research has to be just one of several functions an individual has to carry out. This need not necessarily mean that it will be carried out less efficiently, but it will almost certainly mean that such a researcher will not be as widely experienced as the full-time researcher, and will be hampered by her other commitments. So, though experience of other functions can certainly be useful, if only to remind you that words are important too, those planning to specialise in picture research should make their first aim a job as a full-time researcher.

What jobs are available?

There is no generally recognised avenue of recruitment. Some vacancies are advertised in the press, the weekly *Bookseller* and *The Times Literary Supplement* being two favoured media. The *SPREd Newsletter* (see 1.07) carries information about vacancies known to them, and also general information about new firms' projects for which staff may have to be recruited.

Apart from that, there's no alternative to going the rounds, writing or 'phoning as applicable. If a particular post is advertised, a 'phone call is in order to find out if a vacancy still exists and to make brief inquiries, but you will probably need to follow this up with a letter. If you are making a general application, start with a letter to an individual name, if you know one, or to the Head of the Picture Research Department (titles vary from one firm to another, but that ought to reach him/her).

If you are starting from scratch, the best way to find what firms to apply to is to go along to your nearest bookshop and see what books are being published of the sort you think you could work on, then note the publishers' names. The following is a brief list of British publishers who tend to employ relatively large numbers of full-time picture researchers, but there are very many more:

BPC (British Printing Corporation)	*Mitchell Beazley*
Hamlyn	*Octopus*
Longman	*Orbis*
Macmillan	*Reader's Digest*
Marshall Cavendish	*Weidenfeld & Nicolson*

Applying for a post

It is astonishing how little thought many applicants give to the way in which they make their application, though you'd think it would be obvious to them that they will be judged very sharply on the basis of their application letter.

Unless it's absolutely impossible, your letter should be type-written—and by yourself! Your address and 'phone number should be clearly written, your name not just a scrawled signature but written out in full.

While your letter should not be too long—the reader is likely to be a busy person—it should be packed with information, such as:

● Your age
● Your education, including subjects in which you have passed examinations, and any specialist fields
● Any extracurricular training or qualifications
● Any experience (not necessarily in picture research: for instance, a spell of reporting for your local newspaper would sound well)
● Areas of special interest
● A sentence or two saying briefly why you think you are fitted for the work—why you want to do it—what makes you think you'd be good at it
● Your availability, both for interviews and for starting work.

Book publishers

By far the largest employers of picture researchers are book publishers. The big general publishers, such as those listed above, will give you a breadth of experience unmatched in smaller houses: the smaller publishers will give you a greater opportunity for personal involvement and initiative. Working with a team of colleagues on an encyclopedia or a partwork has one kind of appeal; chasing highly specialised illustrations for scholarly or academic treatises, under the personal guidance of an author, offers another. Ultimately it is a matter of taste. Whichever you choose, you can always switch jobs later, so it doesn't really matter where you start: it's all valuable experience!

Magazine publishers

Working for periodical publications has its own special excitement. The satisfaction of seeing the results of your work in print not long after you've done it is rewarding compared with the long-drawn-out business of researching for a book which may not be published for a year or more after you have completed your research assignment and moved on to something new.

Magazine work can mean a wide variety of work, too, particularly if it's for a weekly like *TV Times* or one of the Sunday supplements: they will give you a greater insight into the business than perhaps any other branch of the profession. At the same time, it is apt to be hectic: you never seem to have enough time to do the job as well as you'd like, there's often the frustration of getting, not the best picture, but the one that's most immediately accessible. However, this too is a challenge, and a researcher can take pride in getting the best possible picture in the shortest possible time.

The big periodical publishing groups such as IPC employ a large number of people on picture research. On smaller periodicals, such as *New Society*, picture research tends to be done by the art editor or his assistants, rather than by a researcher employed for that purpose only. Researchers are generally assigned to a particular periodical, though some groups have research teams who find material for a number of publications—thus if you go to work for *Macmillan Journals* you may find yourself researching for *Nature* one day, *Nursing Times* the next.

Television

All television companies have a department concerned with picture research, though it is often allied with other functions. The BBC obtains nearly all its still pictures through its Central Stills department, and has a separate department for obtaining film material and another for the BBC's own photos. In most of the independent companies picture research is a function of the Library—this is true, for instance, of Thames, Yorkshire and Granada. (Note that the *Radio*

Times Hulton Picture Library, though part of the BBC organisation, is for all practical purposes an independent institution.)

In some respects working for television combines the excitement of working for a magazine with the longer-term opportunities of book research. Many TV programmes are months, sometimes years in the making, and research can often be conducted on a very thorough basis: this is helped by the comparatively large budgets which are available. Against this must be set the occupational hazard of the television business—the scrapping of a project or a complete change in its direction, with the result that a higher proportion of picture research comes to nothing in this than in any other field. And even if all comes to glorious fruition, you will have no souvenir in the form of a handsome printed book—you'll be lucky if your name is listed in the credits.

Advertising agencies, public relations, design studios, and so on

The opportunities for picture researchers in commercial firms differ in one important respect: a very high proportion of the pictures are likely to be specially commissioned, so that the researcher—who is often called the Art Buyer—will spend perhaps the majority of her time briefing photographers or artists. This has its own special appeal, a more direct and creative function: research consists in finding the right photographer or artist rather than the right picture source, though of course most companies will also make use of stock photos and stills. Working conditions are likely to be better than with publishers and magazines, and salaries higher to match the greater responsibility. To be an art buyer for an advertising agency is a very demanding but often exciting job, working as an accepted member of the team and with the chance of enjoying a good deal of personal satisfaction.

Jobs in the field are advertised in the trade weekly *Campaign*.

Visual aids, audiovisual, and so on

The business of providing visual aids—material for audiovisual presentations, educational aids, slide kits, wallcharts and so on—is a rapidly growing one: as yet, however, the opportunities it offers the picture researcher are limited and most work is on a freelance basis. At present the industry is too small for any clear guidelines to have emerged, and the degree of responsibility given to the researcher is liable to vary even more than in other branches of picture research. So, while it is well worth your while to investigate any vacancies in this field, make sure that the work you will be required to perform is appropriate to your abilities and experience. By and large, the work is likely to be much the same as for a book publisher, and if the firm is a producer of, say, educational visual aids on a variety of subjects, research can be as varied and interesting as in any other branch.

1.05 Career Opportunities (2) Freelance

Do not consider working as a freelance researcher until you have gained some experience as a staff researcher, for two reasons:

- Your potential employers will want some assurance that you can be entrusted with a freelance commission
- You yourself will need all the confidence that only past experience can give you.

A freelance researcher is a special breed of person. Unless you are that kind of person, you will do far better not to attempt it. The attractions of independence are counterweighted by a lack of security and a burden of individual responsibility which don't worry some people but depress others intolerably: you will have to find out to which of these categories you belong.

As a freelance, you will be taking on a complex range of activities and responsibilities apart from the research itself. Consider these factors:

- You will have to organise your working day, your office premises, your message-taking facilities, and so on
- You will have to manage your own finances, or arrange for someone else to do so—at *your* expense!
- You will be involved in all sorts of expenditure on letterhead, reference books, files, 'phone, typewriter, and so on
- You will be responsible for obtaining every individual assignment yourself
- You will have to face the fact that when you don't work you don't eat; that there will be no holidays with pay; that if you are ill, all you will have to live on is your national insurance
- There is nobody to protect you against rogues and scoundrels except yourself; you will have to chase slow payers and non-payers yourself.

On the other hand . . .

The advantages of freelance working are evident enough. You work when and how you wish; you don't have to clock in anywhere, or put up with uncongenial colleagues, and you dictate your own work-pattern. You can choose which firms to work for, and which assignments to take on. You will acquire a wider range of experience, and you will almost certainly live a more out-and-about existence. It will be a lot more exhausting and a lot more fun.

The biggest factor of all, the one that is both the attraction and the terror, is that you will personally be 100 per cent responsible for your success or failure. Unless you have real confidence in your own ability, you will not succeed. If you see this as alarming, you had better not try it—or wait until you feel more confident. If you see it as a stimulating challenge, then you're probably the stuff that freelances are made of.

How do you start?

If you have been working within a company, you may well have made contacts within that company which will encourage them to go on employing you on a part-time or assignment basis. Alternatively, you may have made some outside contact which will ensure a basic minimum of work. It is certainly best to start with some kind of 'banker'—an assignment of some duration, or better still a regular retainer, which will pay the rent for the first few months. You would in any case be taking a big chance if you started freelancing without having made some good contacts with potential employers.

Making your existence known

Clearly one of your first concerns will be to tell all your potential employers that you are now available for freelance work. Telephone calls and letters, as appropriate, can be supplemented with a small leaflet or handout giving a few details for those who don't know you—titles of books you've researched, firms you've worked for, special fields of knowledge. You can type this out, even adding a photo of yourself if you think that will help, then have copies duplicated.

Advertising is costly, so you should invest in it only when you're pretty sure your ad will be read by the right people. Two low-cost places are the newsletters of *SPREd* and *BAPLA* (see 1.07) where for a pound or two you can supply information about yourself to likely employers. Apart from that, direct mailing is likely to be most cost-effective.

You should also make friends with as many picture sources as you can, letting them know of your availability, for they are often asked to recommend researchers. If they know you personally they will know what sort of assignments you are likely to be good at and how you will suit a particular client. Apart from that, it is well to maintain good relations with picture sources and keep in personal contact with them as much as possible. Remember that, however friendly they may be disposed to you, they are always going to be slightly on their guard with an individual rather than with the employee of a big firm where the boss can be contacted if there is any bother. You need to impress those you deal with, displaying efficiency and reliability. Good personal relationships are essential to the freelance's success.

Organising yourself

A freelance picture researcher is a one-person business. A very high degree of organisation is called for, and if you're not good at organising yourself you'd do better to stay in a firm and let someone else organise you. The following are just some of the items you'll have to arrange.

Working premises

According to circumstances, these will comprise a room set aside in your house or apartment; an office in the centre of town; or desk space in someone else's office. If you use your own home, it's best to keep your work space separate from your other activities if you can.

Message-taking facilities

Basically, this means the constant availability of a 'phone, with someone at the end of it. It can be someone in the house who's willing, or a telephone answering system. You can instruct the Post Office to transfer 'phone calls, on your instructions, to any number you specify, but this must be by prior arrangement. To inquire about this, dial 100 and ask for 'Transfer Service'. The cost is quite reasonable.

Parcel receiving and sending

Make sure you've got a letterbox big enough to receive the kind of parcels you'll be receiving. It's wise to have an arrangement with a neighbour who'll take in bulkier parcels when you're not there. The postman is usually prepared to be helpful—especially if you remember him generously at Christmas time.

Keep a stock of Jiffybags for returning pictures or sending them on to clients. These are horribly expensive bought one by one from your friendly neighbourhood stationer, incomparably cheaper if bought by the thousand. Trouble is, you don't need a thousand—but if you've got a good relationship going with a picture library, as recommended earlier, maybe they'd let you have 100 at wholesale price.

Don't forget to keep all recorded-delivery slips. Record all postage in a special book. And scales are probably worth investing in if you do a lot of parcel sending.

Stationery

You will need your own letterhead and, if you can afford it, a business card with your name and address. It looks professional.

Typewriter

You must be able to type, even if only with a few of your fingers: if you can't, go to evening classes and learn. Get a typewriter, if possible an electric one. You may be lucky enough to find a good reconditioned or secondhand one—but insist on a guarantee if you do!

Picture storage

Invest in an A4 filing cabinet, four-drawer, and preferably with a lock. Make sure it's fitted for suspended files, which you should also have. You may be able to find this secondhand, also.

Files

You will need files for each individual assignment, files for correspondence, files for invoices, files for your financial documents, files for delivery notes, files for sources' rates cards and conditions, files for catalogues, files for every aspect of your life.

Access to photostat facility

Find out where the nearest one is, note its hours and what fancy services it offers besides straightforward statting. There are cheap home models on the market, but at the present state of technology they're not reckoned a very good buy.

Expense records

Keep a note of everything—every cab, every tube journey, every stamp,

every 'phone call, every parking fee (and fine!). Keep receipts whenever your can. There's a handy device called Monitel which, as it's
name implies, monitors your telephone calls and automatically tells
you the cost. If you do a lot of 'phoning (and what researcher
doesn't?) it could be a useful money-saving device.

Insurance

See 3.10

Finance

You will have to keep good records of all your financial dealings.
Unquestionably you should find a professional accountant to advise
you on the mysteries of VAT, income tax, national insurance and
other nasty matters. Accountants don't come cheap, but almost
always they more than pay their own cost in what they save you by
their advice and by making sure you don't pay any more tax than you
need.

You will do well, when you set up as a freelance, to make a date
with your bank manager and tell him what you're doing. Yours is a
profession in which income will fluctuate—you will receive periodic
payments, hopefully fairly substantial, with gaps in between. Prepare him to expect this, then he'll be sympathetic if you run into a
temporary bad patch. All professional people like to be kept
informed, so always keep in touch. Most publishers pay only at the
end of an assignment, unless it's a very long-drawn-out affair in
which case they should be willing to make interim payments. But
you must be prepared to wait for payment, and so you should really
start with enough money to keep you housed and fed for three
months with nothing coming in. Ideally you should for ever after
have that much set aside for rainy days, but I never yet met a researcher who managed it . . .

More about the financial aspect in 3.05.

Daily record

Most fundamental of all is to keep a daily check on your work—the
pictures you find, the pictures you send on to your employer, the
pictures you get back, the pictures you return. This daily record, in
whatever form you keep it, is at the heart of your business. The
golden rule to keep to right from the start is this: *make a note of everything, at the earliest possible moment.*

Teaming up

There have been periodic attempts to set up freelance picture research agencies, but none has ever achieved any degree of permanent
success. Most businesses describing themselves as if they are picture
research agencies turn out to consist basically of one person with perhaps a secretary and a junior associate. No doubt it's only a matter of
time before such an agency gets off the ground successfully, but it is
not certain that it would be such a good idea. The biggest thing the
individual freelance researcher has to offer is her own personal skill
and experience.

On the other hand there is much to be said in favour of a limited
degree of cooperation. Pooling work, for instance, to the extent that if
one of you is going off to the British Museum this morning on her
own affairs, she can look out pictures for the other members of the
pool: but this can lead to delicate questions of finance, and mutual
recriminations as to whether each member of the pool is pulling her
weight.

What is perhaps more to the point is a sharing of facilities—desk,
'phone, typewriter and so on. Whereas office premises are probably
beyond the means of an individual, two or three banding together
could perhaps afford them.

1.06 Career Opportunities (3) Art Libraries and Picture Sources

Many of the qualifications for being a picture researcher are equally
suitable for working in an art library or some other picture source:
and since a large part of an art librarian's work consists of locating
and researching pictures within the library, it could be said that the
job itself is largely similar. On the other hand the circumstances in
which the job is carried out, located in a single place and often con-
fined to a limited range of material, would seem to suit a different
temperament.

However, there is clearly a large overlap of skills and, temperament apart, it is probably fair to say that most researchers would
make fair librarians and most librarians fair researchers. It is true
that many picture libraries expect to recruit staff with some formal
library training or experience, but this is by no means always the
case, particularly with the less institutional picture sources, where

knowledge and experience are valued more highly than formal training.

Furthermore, it is being widely recognised, even within the library profession, that picture libraries are very different from book libraries, and that the rigid application to pictures of standard systems and methods designed for books is often impracticable. None the less, while the more enlightened art libraries will not necessarily look on professional library training as indispensable, it continues to be better to have the letters ALA after your name than not!

Ideally it would be possible to combine the jobs of librarian and researcher, in a source where there is also a research facility, or where the functions of the library make research part of the job; or simply by arrangement, such as one London researcher who works four days a week in a picture library but does freelance research the rest of the time—with the knowledge and indeed encouragement of her employers. The experience of visiting other picture sources is vital to any librarian, and it is significant that *ARLIS*—the *Art Libraries Society*—organises such visits to spread awareness of alternative methods among its members. The occupational disease of all libraries is a rigid faith that their own ways are the best ways, and this is the sort of state of mind which can dampen the enthusiasm of those who join the profession.

At its best, however, working in a picture source can be a stimulating and rewarding job. The facts that you are concerned with supply rather than demand and are not involved in the creative work of book or TV programme production don't mean that the maintenance and building-up of a picture stock are not also satisfying and creative. In particular, gathering and collecting a specialist collection of material on, say, local topography has its own very strong appeal.

Working for a picture source is as good or as bad as the source itself makes it, and as we shall see in Part Two of this guide sources can vary enormously. In a Fleet Street press agency you are working in what is to all intents the department of a newspaper office; in a historical loan collection you are virtually working in a museum; in an art library you are virtually working in a public library; in a stock photo library you are virtually working in the art department of an advertising agency. And, just as the places themselves vary with their functions, so do their working conditions. Some are impersonal and functional, others homely and messy; some big and rough, others small and cosy. In some you will meet your clients and help them with their problems—which is of course very enjoyable if you like that side of the work, but irritating if you're longing to get on with something else. In some you'll be stuck behind a desk all day; in others you'll switch from making the tea to dry-mounting photos to filing returned pictures to typing captions to 'phoning New York to popping over to the Post Office with a registered packet and would you be an angel and pick up some prints from the photographer's on your way back . . . The only way to find out whether you'd like to work in a particular place is to know them in the first place, and the best way to do that is start by visiting them as a picture researcher.

'Library' or 'supplier'?

If you decide to work for a picture source, you had better decide fairly early on whether you want to work for one which is more of a library than a supplier, or vice versa.

On the one hand there's the kind of picture archive which is primarily a collection, and where the loan facilities are secondary. For this type of work, you will certainly do well to acquire some kind of professional library qualifications in the course of your training, and there is less advantage in obtaining practical research experience. This would apply to, say, working for the *National Maritime Museum* or for a polytechnic art library. Professional library qualifications cover all aspects of librarianship, and usually comprise taking the examinations of the *Library Association*, for which you would study at one of the recognised Schools of Librarianship throughout the country. For details, write to the Library Association, 7 Ridgmount St, London WC1E 7AE, for their leaflet 'How to become a Chartered Librarian'.

On the other hand, if you opt for the kind of picture source whose primary function is lending material—one which probably exists only for that purpose—such as a Fleet Street press agency or a historical collection like the *Mary Evans Picture Library*, then formal library training is probably less important. It will be valuable, and certainly stand you in good stead when you apply for a job, but practical experience in the research field will also be sought. For, until you know what the problems are, how can you know how to solve them?

1.07 Professional Organisations

There are many professional and other related organisations whose activities may be of interest to the picture researcher. Some you will want to join, some you may look to for help and advice, others you simply need to be aware of. If you want to know more, write to the Secretary at the address given.

American Society of Picture Professionals (ASPP)
Box 5283, Grand Central Station, New York, NY 10017, USA

The essential organisation for American picture researchers. Unlike SPREd it also includes photographers and others in the picture business. Regular meetings and social activities, newsletter and other publications. Liaises with SPREd, so if you need American contacts, information, and so on this can be managed via SPREd.

Art Libraries Society (ARLIS)
Secretary: Gillian Varley, Kingston Polytechnic, Knights Park, Kingston, Surrey

Essential organisation for all on the art library side of picture research. Primary function is disseminating information among members via bi-monthly newsletter and quarterly journal, and sponsoring occasional larger publications such as Philip Pacey's *Art Library Manual* (see 1.08). Occasional meetings and visits.

Association Nationale des Journalistes, Reporters, Photographes et Cinéastes (ANJRPC)
24 rue du Laos, Paris 75015

French organisation of picture sources, to which most leading photo agencies belong. Issues recommended rates and conditions along the same lines as BAPLA, IIP, AFAEP, etc., in Britain.

Association of Fashion, Advertising and Editorial Photographers (AFAEP)
10a Dryden Street, London WC2E 9NA

Recommends fees and codes of practice, model terms of employment, negotiates with government bodies, trade unions and so on, on behalf of members. Provides information on stylists, home economists, set builders, studio register, assistants freelance and permanent. Group facilities and insurance etc. No services open to non-member photographers other than initial contact.

Four ways of looking at a
subject: *above*, a straight
photograph of the ageing
Victoria; *right*, a prestige
etching; *overleaf above*, an artist's
view (William Nicholson); and,
overleaf below, a more critical
satirical comment (*Funny Folks*,
1886)

Association pour la Diffusion des Arts Graphiques et Plastiques (ADAGP)

French organisation for handling the copyright of a number of artists. Agents for the UK are Everett Pinto & Co., Chile House, 20/24 Ropemaker Street, London EC2Y 9AT (Phone 01–628 3152) who also represent SPADEM (see below). Apply to them for list of affiliated artists, details of copyright fees, etc.

British Association of Picture Libraries and Agencies (BAPLA)
PO Box 93 London NW6 5XW

Most of the more important British commercial picture sources, and many of the non-commercial ones, are members of this association which disseminates information, establishes codes of working practice and recommends minimum rates. There are periodic meetings and a newsletter. Co-operates with SPREd on matters of mutual interest.

Bundesverband der Pressebild-Agenturen, Bilderdienste und Bildarchive
Secretary: Friedrich Rauch, Maximilianstrasse 15, 8000 München 22, Germany.

German association of picture sources, including most of the major commercial collections. Deliberately keeps its numbers limited. Monthly newsletter, much more serious and formal than its English-speaking equivalents.

Council of Photographic News Agencies (CPNA)
Bath House, Holborn Viaduct, London EC1   01–248 5550

Most press agencies, including picture sources in the news agency field, belong to this professional organisation which has established a code of working practice and recommends minimum rates.

Courtauld Institute of Art
20 Portman Square, London W1H OBE   01–935 9292

Part of the University of London. Among varied activities, the Institute runs courses in European Art History which are probably the finest formal training a picture researcher could hope to receive. These may be taken either as three-year undergraduate courses for BA, or as postgraduate courses (one or two years according to previous qualifications) for MA, MPhil, PhD and other courses.

The Ephemera Society
12 Fitzroy Square, London W1P 5AH   01–387 7723

Though not all the members of this society make their material available to researchers, many do: between them they have astonishing collections, private or institutional, covering a dazzling range of material. Their periodic exhibitions are a 'must' for researchers.

Institute of Incorporated Photographers (IIP)
2 Amwell End, Ware, Hertfordshire SG12 9HN   Ware 4011

Association of professional photographers. Meetings, monthly journal, and—of particular interest to researchers—register of members (copy available on request). An essential source of information on all matters relating to professional photography. Code of fair practice, recommended minimum rates.

Institute of Journalists
1 Whitehall Place, London SW1A 2HE   01–930 7441

Professional organisation for journalists, including freelances. Employment register.

The Library Association
7 Ridgmount Street, London WC1E 7AE   01–636 7543

The central information source for all matters relating to libraries and librarianship. Its professional qualifications for Chartered Librarians are the accepted standard (see 1.06). The reference library (part of the British Library) is open to the public, and includes, among a great deal of specialised literature, all available reference works on libraries so that a researcher can easily check on likely sources. Pleasant reading room and helpful staff.

The Museums Association
87 Charlotte Street, London W1P 2BX   01–636 4600

The central information source on all matters relating to museums, including working in them. Has published a number of excellent information sheets of interest to researchers (see 1.08). Offers qualifications in the form of diploma courses.

The National Book League
7 Albermarle Street, London W1X 4BB   01–493 9001

Promotes interest in books by means of exhibitions, prizes and publications. The Mark Longman Library contains some 10,000 books about books, one of the best reference sources of its kind, and there is a Readers' Information Service. The library is open to the public, but only members can take books away. It issues many publications listing selected books in specific fields, which could be of interest to the researcher.

The National Union of Journalists (NUJ)
314 Grays Inn Road, London WC1X 8DP   01–278 7916

The trade union favoured by most picture researchers who feel the need for union solidarity. Has a freelance branch. Seeks to establish agreement about minimum rates and conditions.

The Photographers' Gallery
8 Great Newport Street, London WC2   01–240 1969

Essential place for all picture researchers to keep their eye on, with its regular exhibitions and its wide range of relevant publications. There is a slide collection comprising the work of important photographers, and the staff are a mine of useful information.

The Publishers Association
19 Bedford Square, London WC1B 3HJ   01–580 6321

Membership includes most of the leading British publishers. Its chief interest for the researcher is that it occasionally holds short courses in picture research, one of the very few attempts at formal training in this field. Unfortunately these courses are infrequent and available only to the staff of member organisations.

The Royal Photographic Society
14 South Audley Street, London W1Y 5DP   01–493 3967

Besides being a valuable source of photographic material, particularly historical, the RPS has a very extensive library on photography, and this, combined with the knowledge of its staff, is an invaluable source of information for researchers. The Society plans to open the RPS National Photographic Centre in Bath, with the cooperation of the University of Bath, which will comprise a photograph gallery, museum, research centre and educational unit.

The Society of Photographers in Communications Inc (ASMP)
60 East 42nd Street, New York, NY 10017, USA

Has established guidelines for working practice and suggests minimum rates. The *ASMP Guide to Business Practices in Photography* is essential reference for all researchers doing business with America.

(Virtually any professional organisation in this country, such as BAPLA or SPREd, will have a copy you can examine.)

Société de la Propriété Artistique et des Dessins et Modèles (SPADEM)

French organisation for the protection of copyright of artistic work. Details similar to ADAGP above.

Society of Picture Researchers and Editors (SPREd)
c/o National Westminster Bank, 110 Wardour Street, London W1

Last on our list, but first in importance for the British picture researcher, this is the essential professional organisation for both staff and freelance researchers. Establishes code of practice, advises on dealing with employers and picture sources, co-operates with NUJ and other unions, also with BAPLA, AFAEP and other organisations. Meetings, talks, visits, periodic newsletter. Liaises with ASPP and other overseas organisations. Training courses for researchers are a hoped-for future development.

1.08 Reference Books

The following list of books is, inevitably, a personal choice, for ultimately almost any book can be of some value. Some of these a picture researcher should either own or at any rate have constant and immediate access to; some she should simply be aware of; with others, such as encyclopedias, she should determine the most convenient location where they may be consulted at a moment's notice.

Directories and books on research

With the possible exception of the four foreign directories, and of *Treasures of Britain* if this doesn't happen to be your field, in my opinion all books in this section are essential for every researcher to own or have constant access to.

Directory of British Photographic Collections, compiled by John Wall for the Royal Photographic Society, and published by Heinemann for the National Photographic Record. Despite many omissions, bewildering arrangement and some of the worst proof-reading in the history of publishing, this is a useful address-book (though many addresses are now out of date) simply on account of its scope.

Historic Houses, Castles and Gardens in Great Britain and Ireland, published annually by ABC Historic Publications every October and obtainable from most booksellers. An astonishingly good publication, packed with solid information, and at a very modest price.

Lexicon der Farbfoto Archive, Verlag Presse, Baden Baden, West Germany. An impressive if somewhat daunting German compilation which sets out to give the inventory of 2,417 sources of colour pictures: the subject references number more than 10,000. Though out of date even before publication, it is none the less an important international research tool.

Major Libraries of the World, by Colin Steele of the Bodleian Library, published by Bowker. A superbly produced and informative guide to 300 major libraries throughout the world, giving details not only of collections but also toilet and snack facilities. Unfortunately it does not cover picture availability and copying facilities.

Museums and Galleries in Great Britain and Ireland. Another excellent ABC Historic publication, even more indispensable.

Picture Researcher's Handbook, by Hilary & Mary Evans. New edition 1979 obtainable from Mary Evans Picture Library or from Saturday Ventures, 11 Granville Park, London SE13 7DY. An international guide to the world's most useful picture sources, with comprehensive information and cross indexes. An indispensable guide which every researcher should possess.

Picture Sources 3, compiled by Ann Novotny and Rosemary Eakins for the American Special Libraries Association, 1975. An in-depth directory of American picture sources, essential for any researcher doing business in or with America.

Répertoire des Collections Photographiques en France. The definitive guide to French picture sources. A new edition is scheduled for 1979. Information is briefer than in the two preceding books; but this is an essential for a researcher doing much work in or with France.

Research, by Ann Hoffmann, (Midas Books, 12 Dene Way, Speldhurst, Tunbridge Wells, Kent TN3 0NX). Though intended primarily for the writer, this book is packed with solid information which is also of value to the picture researcher, and there is an appendix on Picture Research by Pat Hodgson. A very useful source of facts.

Stock Photo and Assignment Source Book, edited by Fred W. McDarragh (Bowker 1977). This is potentially a useful book, in that it sets out to list not only straightforward picture sources but also individual photographers, business sources, official and public information sources etc. Unfortunately the information is very heavily weighted with American sources, and the book is carelessly compiled (on at least two occasions sources are listed twice due to misprints), out of date already, and expensive.

Treasures of Britain, AA/Reader's Digest. Despite its 'coffee-table' appearance, this book contains much useful information about what's where in stately homes and other collections, and, though not as factual as *Historic Houses*, complements it with greater detail.

The Writer's and Artist's Yearbook, annually from A & C Black. An essential working tool for the researcher, giving the addresses of most publishers and periodicals, selected picture sources, agencies, institutions, etc.

Reference books you should own or have access to

A selective suggestions-list for day-to-day fact-finding.

People

The best biographical dictionary is *Webster's*, superbly produced, one of the things the Americans do better than anyone, but dates should be independently checked. International scope. Useful tables—like lists of Prime Ministers of Venezuela. For more detail on British people, the *Concise Dictionary of National Biography*, one volume to 1900, another for people who have died since then. *Hyamson's Dictionary of Universal Biography* (Routledge), though containing many inaccuracies, gives one-line descriptions which are just enough to identify the person, which means they can pack in far more names than any other. Essential for historical researchers. The *British Museum Catalogue of Engraved British Portraits* is a very good source of obscure information about people whose names do not appear in other books because they did little of note, but did have their portrait done; in particular, wives of great men, countesses and duchesses.

Places

Webster's Geographical Dictionary is indispensable, despite its irritating practice of putting American places first, so that Athens, Arkansas, precedes the Greek city of the same name . . . Chauvinism apart, an excellent reference work. The *Times Atlas of the World* is unrivalled, and well worth saving up for. The *Reader's Digest Atlas* is, like all their books, excellently produced, but doesn't really contain enough detail; their *Atlas of Great Britain*, on the other hand, is a very useful volume to own.

Events

For historical events, nobody has ever bettered *Haydn's Dictionary of Dates*: well worth looking out for a secondhand copy even though it hasn't been published since the beginning of the century. Penguin and Dent (Everyman) have both tried to bring out a modern equivalent, but I haven't found either of them really satisfactory. Other nineteenth-century books worth picking up if you can are *Brewer's Historical Dictionary* (with a very handy list of battles) and his *Reader's Companion*, both packed with the sort of elusive facts it's so difficult to track down. Again, these can be found only in secondhand shops.

Languages

You should have dictionaries of the main foreign languages if you do any overseas business or have to obtain material from abroad. There is plenty of choice, but I recommend: French—Harrap's; German—Langenscheidt's; Italian—Cassell's.

Literature

The various *Oxford Companions*—to English, French, German and American literature and also their *Classical Dictionary*—are unmatched in this field. However, the equivalent *Penguin Companions* are also good and, of course, much cheaper.

Miscellaneous

No household is complete without *Brewer's Dictionary of Phrase & Fable* for its wealth of trivia and sheer serendipity. Arthur Mee's amazing *I See All*, produced back in the 'twenties, has a unique place on the reference shelf because it shows everything in tiny little pictures—usually awful—showing you just what a bowsprit is, or a serif or a quern. Why no enterprising publisher has brought out an up-to-date version is understandable, considering the unbelievable amount of work that must have gone into it, but you'd think someone would have the courage . . .

For music, you can't unfortunately do better than the appalling *Oxford Companion to Music*, the most ill-contrived reference book on any major theme and surely due for replacement any day now? Their *Companion to Art*, on the other hand, is a useful volume when you don't want to be bothered with the many more comprehensive reference books available.

Books on specialist aspects of the researcher's work

Once again, a very selective list of books that I have personally found useful.

Art libraries

Art Library Manual, edited by Philip Pacey, produced by Bowker in association with ARLIS, 1977. Chapters on many aspects of the Art Librarian's work, including many subjects of wider interest.

Art techniques

The Complete Book of Artists' Techniques, Kurt Herberts, Thames & Hudson, 1958. A magnificently lucid presentation of the various techniques used by artists from prehistoric cave paintings to today's acrylic resins. The author is also concerned to show technique as a means to an end—*why* did one era prefer silverpoint while another preferred red chalk? Splendidly enlightening for the researcher concerned with art subjects.

Art reproductions

The UNESCO Catalogue of Colour Reproductions of Paintings, though inevitably out of date before publication, is a valuable indicator when tracking down works of art.

Copyright

Copyright Law Concerning Works of Art, Photographs and the Written and Spoken Word, by Charles Gibbs-Smith, for the Museums Association, Information Sheet 7, revised 1974. A brave and brilliant attempt to reduce the complexities of copyright to fourteen lucid jargon-free pages. Vital reading for every researcher. Obtainable from the Museums Association, 87 Charlotte St, London W1P 2BX.

Ephemera

Printed Ephemera, by John Lewis, Faber, 1969. A superb introduction to the variety of material available in this field.

Illustration

Sources of Illustration, 1500–1900, Hilary and Mary Evans, Adams & Dart, 1972. Surveys the various forms of illustration and reproduction in the pre-photographic era. Prepared with the picture researcher in mind, so not overburdened with technicalities. Practical descriptions explain techniques in not too much detail. Because the subject of the book is illustrations, the book is packed with them.

Learning

World of Learning, published biennially by Europa. An international guide to museums, learned societies, universities, galleries, etc. An important reference source.

Portraits

ALA Portrait Index, published for the Library of Congress in 1906. Another of those vital reference works which no publisher has had the courage to up-date: still an important information source.

Press

Willings' Press Guide. Annual directory of British and principal overseas publications.

Printing

Printing Processes, by David Carey, Ladybird Books, 1971. Don't laugh—this book aimed at children does a superb job of getting over the basic principles of printing, and if you need an introduction to the various processes, this makes an excellent starting point.

A Guide to Printing, William Clowes, Heinemann, 1963. There are many books about printing, but this is a well written, lucid and fact-packed guide which makes a good second-stage read when you've mastered the basics described in the previous book.

Reproduction fees

Reproduction Fees, Photography, Etc.: Guidelines for Museums. Another of the Museums Association's excellent Information Sheets. Despite its title, this twelve-page leaflet discusses many wider issues with lucidity and authority, and should be required reading for every picture researcher and every picture source as well as every museum curator.

Reproduction techniques

The Graphic Reproduction and Photography of Works of Art, John Lewis and Edwin Smith, W. S. Cowell, 1969, distributed by Faber & Faber. The cumbersome title sums up the scope of this handsome and uniquely informative book which, though full of technical information, contains a good deal of general material to interest the researcher.

1.09 Libraries

Libraries of interest to the picture researcher may be usefully classified as 'convenient', 'indispensable', 'in-depth' or 'specialist'. The following list can only be selective:

'Convenient' libraries

Every researcher needs a library she can pop into quickly when she needs to know something fast, like where Timbuktu is or the date of the Battle of Plassey, the 'phone number of the NAACP and what in heaven's name is the Unified Field Theory? This means, really, an open access library where you can get at the books without having to order them and wait while someone brings them to you.

For most purposes your local public library will meet your needs. Most have a basic reference collection and the staff are usually ready to help if you get stuck. If you need more than a brief reference and they don't have the book you need, they can usually obtain it for you via Interlibrary Loan as part of their regular service. Most public libraries have one field in which they specialise, and the London libraries in particular are formally organised so as to distribute responsibility for particular areas of interest; e.g., medicine at Marylebone (in the Marylebone Road), foreign language books at Mayfair (South Audley Street), fine arts at Westminster (see below) and

English literature at Victoria (Buckingham Palace Road).

To walk out of the glare and glitter of Leicester Square into the *Central Reference Library* in St Martin's Street, WC2, is an astonishing experience. Here in this central location is an almost unbelievable array of reference books, many thousands on open access, on every conceivable subject, including all the standard works and many you probably didn't know existed—like the American *Who knows what?*, a directory of experts in scientific and other fields of specialist knowledge. Hours are 10 to 7 Monday to Friday, 10 to 5 on Saturday.

Most major cities have their equivalent, and it is worth while familiarising yourself with its contents and arrangement; for instance, when you have a few minutes to spare between engagements. Knowledge of the arrangement may save you time one day when you're in a hurry!

With so much available from public sources, it might seem superfluous to pay the annual subscription (£36 in 1978) to the *London Library*; even though it's tax-deductible, that's a lot to spend. Yet most freelance researchers find it worthwhile joining, and I doubt if there's a single picture research department in any organisation that hasn't a corporate membership. The reason is that there you not only have direct access to a vast quantity of books on every subject, including great runs of periodicals, but can borrow up to ten titles at one time (more by arrangement). With its central location and its seldom crowded reading room, not to mention its unique atmosphere, it is a very convenient place indeed. For details, write to the Librarian, 14 St James's Square, London SW1Y 4LG. Opening hours are 9.30 to 5.30 Monday to Saturday, late opening to 7.30 on Thursday.

Remember, moreover, that many libraries which don't offer open access for the bulk of their material, do so for their reference material; so if you live just round the corner from, say, the *Victoria & Albert Museum*, you can make use of their library facilities in this way.

'Indispensable' libraries

These are the libraries which possess books that nobody else does. First in importance, inevitably, is the *British Library*, still housed in the British Museum, Great Russell Street. Its enormous bulk makes it inevitably unwieldy, and you will undoubtedly spend many frustrating hours within its walls: but the authorities have made great efforts to make its contents accessible and its procedure comprehensible—there is a twenty-page *Notes for Readers* to help you understand how it all works—and the staff do their best to be helpful.

However, they are keen to advise you to try to find what you want elsewhere first, and come to them only if you really need to.

You will need a Reader's Ticket, for which you will need an Application Form, for which you must write to the Keeper of Printed Books, stating briefly why you need to use the library. If your application is accepted, you will receive a ticket—free of charge—with your photograph on it to identify you. Opening hours are 9 to 5 daily, to 9 on Tuesday, Wednesday and Thursday.

A small number of periodicals (listed in *Notes for Readers*) are kept at the British Library, but the bulk of them are at the *Newspaper Library* at Colindale Avenue, NW9. Opening hours are 10 to 5, Monday to Saturday.

Other libraries which come into the 'indispensable' category, depending on where you work, are the *Bodleian Library* at Oxford, and university libraries throughout the country, all of which possess some unique material—at Canterbury, for example, their forte is political caricature.

'In-depth' libraries

There are some libraries which, while not so easy of access as your local public library, enable you to go more deeply into your subject without too much trouble. One example is the *Victoria & Albert Museum Library* which is one of the world's finest art reference libraries: its half million books cover not only all aspects of arts and crafts but a wide range of related subjects. There is a very comprehensive subject index as well as the author and title index. A certain amount of reference material is on open access but the greater part is stacked and brought to you on presentation of an application form: the process is fast and efficient, and the staff helpful. If you want to use it regularly you will need a Reader's Ticket (apply to the Keeper) but you can make occasional use without a ticket.

The *Westminster Fine Arts Library*, two flights above the Central Reference Library in St Martin's Street, Trafalgar Square, has a very convenient art reference collection of some 22,000 books. The standard works are on open access, including many periodicals: others must be requested, but as the stacks are immediately adjacent this is a fairly rapid matter. The collection includes monographs on individual artists, exhibition catalogues and art periodicals. There is a special collection on William Blake and a collection of some 7,000 transparencies of fine art subjects. Hours 10 to 7, Monday to Friday, to 5 on Saturday.

The *Courtauld Institute of Art*, at 20 Portman Square, London W1H 0BE, has, in addition to its other facilities, two important art reference libraries which are both picture sources and unique reference archives: (1) The *Conway Library* is a study collection, created primarily for scholarly research, containing photographs of western architecture, architectural drawings, sculpture, illuminated manuscripts, metalwork, ivories and stained glass. Architectural examples are shown in considerable detail and sculptures are filed both by location and by description—fonts, tombs, etc. (2) The *Witt Library* contains photographs and reproductions of paintings, drawings and engravings in the Western European tradition. This library, too, is primarily for art reference; items are filed under national schools, then by artist's name.

Between them, the two collections contain some 1,200,000 items, mostly in black and white. Their use for reference purposes is free of charge.

Specialist libraries

Most professional bodies and public institutions have their own libraries, to which serious researchers may have access. It is usually prudent to check first what the position is, and whether you need prior permission.

Examples of such libraries are those belonging to the various museums, such as *The Science Museum* and *The Natural History Museum*. One public library of special interest to picture researchers, yet easily overlooked, is the *St Bride Printing Library*, in Bride Lane off Fleet Street, which has a wonderful collection of books relating not only to printing but also to many related subjects. Much of their material has been photographed so that they also constitute a valuable picture source.

Another useful specialist library is that of the Library Association: the *British Library Library Association Library (sic)*. For details see the entry under 'Library Association' in 1.07.

Finally, in this very selective list, the *Guildhall Library* should be mentioned. Its unique book reference collection on the history and topography of London is backed by the collection of prints and drawings which constitutes a very important picture source for the researcher.

PART TWO

PICTURE SOURCES

2.01 Varieties of Picture Source

The primary function of the picture researcher is finding pictures, and this breaks down into two tasks:

- finding a source likely to have the picture(s) you want
- choosing the picture from the selection you are offered

Since the second follows from the first, it is evident that knowing your sources is the most important part of your capability as a researcher.

Finding and choosing sources is largely a question of experience, but not entirely; intuition also plays a part. Even when two sources may have much the same material, there will be differences between them which may prompt you to go to one rather than the other, sometimes as a matter of personal preference but more often because each source has its own individual character and attitude towards its material. Even when, say, two picture agencies hold stock photos of the Taj Mahal, the chances are that one will be a different kind of picture from the other.

Three main categories

Picture sources can be divided into three broad categories:

- *Public collections* Museums, galleries, national and local archives, libraries, collections related to official bodies and authorities, etc.
- *Commercial sources* Press and photo agencies, collections created specifically for loan purposes, individual photographers, commercial press offices and publicity departments, etc.
- *Specialist sources* Learned societies and professional bodies, private collections built up by enthusiasts, colleges and institutions, stately homes, etc.

These are all described in greater detail in the chapters which follow. Each source will, however, differ from others in the same category in respect of such factors as:

- quality and scope of material
- cost of using material
- restrictions on research (e.g., limited to scholarly use)

● quality of service and helpfulness of staff
● delay in obtaining material
● accessibility.

Of these factors, some—such as the quality of the material, limitations on use, and cost—are physical matters you can't do much about: others, such as the quality of the service, are things you'll learn from experience, and which will affect you more or less according to your temperament. Of all the ways in which one source differs from another, accessibility is the most decisive.

Accessibility

Most sources that the professional picture researcher is likely to use will be geared, more or less, to making their material publicly available. But the extent to which they do so can lead to astonishing differences. In this respect, picture sources can be positioned along a scale which is not precisely matched to the three categories already described:

● Sources created for the avowed purpose of supplying pictures. This includes all press and photo agencies, collections such as the *Radio Times Hulton Library* and the *Mansell Collection*, photographic departments of public institutions such as the GLC, commercial publicity departments, etc.
● Sources created primarily as collections, but which reckon to make their material available for reproduction purposes. This includes most public collections and archives, such as the *St Bride Printing Library* or the *Sutcliffe Gallery* at Whitby, and collections in some university departments
● Sources which are neither of the above, but which happen to possess items of interest to a researcher. Thus Kings College, Cambridge, possesses a portrait of the economist Pigou which, to my knowledge, is not available elsewhere.

Clearly these three types of source will require different degrees of effort and initiative from the researcher. The first category will be easy to deal with: there will be a streamlined procedure, printed rates and conditions, informed staff, and the material itself will be organised in the most convenient form for research. All of this will be somewhat less true of those in the second category, which are likely to differ widely one from another depending on how they see their rôle as suppliers as against their rôle as custodians. In the third category, the chances are that the researcher will have to make all the effort: the source may well have no experience whatever of making its material available, and it will be up to the researcher to initiate every step of the procedure.

Nor does accessibility stop there: two sources which are equally geared to making their material available may nevertheless differ over the fundamental question of open access. At the *Radio Times Hulton Picture Library*, for example, researchers do not have direct access to the files: you order your material and a member of the staff brings it to you. At the *Mary Evans Picture Library*, on the other hand, personal research is not only permitted but positively encouraged, on the principle that the researcher knows best what sort of material she is looking for. Each method has its advantages, and it could be said that each of these two libraries is catering for a different kind of client. It is up to you to decide which form of procedure suits you or your current assignment best.

Clearly, accessibility is far from being simply a question of geography. For example, it will often be easier to obtain a picture from a commercial source overseas than from a non-commercial source in the researcher's own city, simply because of the existence or otherwise of the necessary machinery. Where time is important, it is quicker to 'phone Berlin for a picture which can be popped into the post that day and will arrive in London in two or three days than to enter into laborious efforts to obtain the same picture from, say, a run of periodicals which are housed close at hand—from the *Victoria & Albert Museum Library's* run of the *Illustrirte Zeitung*, for instance.

2.02 Public Collections

The vast bulk of historical material tends to be collected in public collections such as the *British Museum* in London, the *Bibliothèque Nationale* in Paris or the *Library of Congress* in Washington. These are supplemented by thousands of less all-embracing collections, ranging from specialist museums such as the *National Maritime Museum* at Greenwich or the *Smithsonian Institute* in Washington to local libraries, university and college collections, and institutions such as the *Peabody Museum* at Salem, Massachusetts. Of course, public collections are not restricted to historical material—take for example NASA, much of whose material is in the form of artists' impressions of *future* events.

These establishments will almost certainly possess the finest available material on their given subjects. But it is important to remember that they are primarily *collections*: that is, their primary function is to collect, preserve and safeguard unique material. Making that material available to the public for inspection and consultation may be an essential part of that function, but making it available for reproduction is generally a secondary matter.

The difficulty commences with the question of how such establishments keep their material and catalogue it. The vast quantities of material possessed by the larger institutions have often been acquired in the form of individual collections, and often remain in them, so that one of the first things you will need to know is that such-and-such an item is not simply in the *Bodleian Library*, say, but specifically in the *John Johnson Collection*. The *Library of Congress*, Washington, is largely composed of separate collections, each of which has its own *raison d'être*.

Typically, in such collections, the material is filed by artist's name rather than by subject, so if what you want is a good picture of a stagecoach interior in the late eighteenth century you will need to know which artist(s) specialised in that type of subject as well as in which special collections that artist's work is to be found.

What this means is that such collections are most useful to the researcher who knows exactly what she is looking for: then her only problem is to locate and obtain it. From this it follows that she will very often be using material which has been used previously, for how else can she know of its existence? If she wants to use fresh material, not previously reproduced, how is she to discover it? Ideally, of course, someone should go through all the illustrated books in the *British Library* and other such collections, noting each item and building up a subject as well as an artist index; then all the researcher would have to do would be to consult all the books—there might well be only a few hundred—which were listed as containing pictures of stagecoaches. But such a subject index does not exist, nor is likely to until the British Library can afford to assign a few dozen full-time cataloguers to the job. In the meantime, the vast bulk of material must remain undiscovered except by the alert or lucky researcher.

Size, in short, is by no means always a blessing. The *John Johnson Collection of Printed Ephemera* at the *Bodleian Library*, referred to above, is almost certainly the finest collection of its kind in the world. But the sheer mass of its material makes research a daunting matter. The historian of, say, trade cards in eighteenth century London will be delighted to have drawers full of the material he wants: but the researcher who simply needs one or two for a social history of the period may be dismayed by so dazzling a choice, and prefer a smaller and more selective collection.

Down-to-earth difficulties

Your problems are far from over when you have tracked down the item you want. To gain access to and sight of the item present further difficulties of a down-to-earth character. For most such collections you will need to obtain a Reader's Ticket. There is usually no great difficulty in obtaining one, but the prudent researcher will make sure of a ticket in advance of her needs, as there may well be some delay between making application and receiving permission. It's no use turning up at, say, the *Bibliothèque Nationale* and hoping to be admitted there and then.

Next, there's the apparently simple matter of finding a seat. All major libraries tend to be overcrowded: at the *British Library* or the *British Museum Print Room*, for example, all seats are likely to be occupied by about 11am. Next, having secured a seat and filled in your application form for the item you want, having located its press number in the catalogue, you have to wait until it is brought to you. Most libraries are extremely efficient, but their sheer size means that such an operation inevitably takes time: when you order a book at the British Library, you are asking for one of 10,000,000 books, so it is bound to take a little while to find the one you want.

Ultimately, however, armed with your ticket, you have gained admission to the collection, secured your place, ordered your item and obtained it. There is the picture you want, right before your eyes. What next? You can't take it away, so the next hurdle is getting it copied.

If you are lucky, it will already have been photographed by some previous researcher, in which case the source itself may have it on negative, in which case all you need do is find out its print number, order a print, and wait. The wait may not be more than a few days, though in practice it is often quite a bit more.

Alternatively, the picture may have been copied by an outside photographer, whose name will appear in the credits if the picture has been reproduced in another book. In this case you can go directly to the photographer and order another print or borrow a transparency (see 3.07), in which case you will have to pay a fee to the source who own the picture as well as one to the photographer who has copied it. (This is something the photographer will be able to tell you about, for, though he took the picture and can lend or sell you a copy, he cannot give you permission to reproduce it—see 2.12.)

More likely, though, you will not want to use a picture which has been used (and perhaps over-used) previously, so it will be a question of having it photographed for the first time. How you do this depends on the institution. Some have an established procedure, and may even have a leaflet telling you, so ask first. The choices are:

● The institution may have its own photographic department which keeps negatives of items already photographed, from which it runs off further copyprints as required, or which undertakes to copy items which have not hitherto been copied. This is fine in principle, but in practice such official departments nearly always have a formidable backlog of work and you will have to be prepared for a delay of two to six weeks or more. The cost, however, is usually very modest.

● Other institutions, while having no photographic department of their own, have a standing arrangement with an outside photographer who makes periodic visits to copy material ordered by researchers or required by the institution itself. This is likely to be a faster process than the one described above, but will be more expensive, though there is usually a fair standard rate agreed with the institution. One drawback is that you may not approve the institution's choice of photographer.

● In the absence of any laid-down procedure, you may be allowed to send in the photographer of your choice. (More about commissioning a photographer in 3.07). He may well have his own arrangements with the institution—there is a lot to be said for using a photographer who is familiar with the place and may even pay regular visits there to copy material, in which case it may not cost so much.

● In some institutions—the Victoria & Albert Museum is an example—they are very permissive about allowing photography and, so long as you ask permission first, will generally allow you to take your own photographs. There is often a distinction between hand-held cameras and tripod-mounted: if you go in with your own small Pentax or whatever, and copy an item without requiring lights, etc., permission is easily obtained, whereas a more formal agreement may be required if you want to carry out a more elaborate job.

Reproduction fees at public collections

There are two schools of thought among museum curators, with regard to reproduction fees.

One school takes the view that since the museums are public property, paid for by the public, their material should in consequence be made available to the public, along with whatever services are called for, and if not free of charge, then at the lowest practicable price.

Others, while not disputing that the public collections have a public responsibility, argue that since most reproduction is for the commercial advantage of the publisher or other user, it is evident that if he obtains his services free, the user is gaining financially at the expense of the rest of the public who would, in effect, be subsidising his commercial venture by allowing him to obtain his material at an unrealistic price.

This latter view is gradually prevailing over the former, and it is becoming generally recognised that the publisher who is using public material for private gain should reimburse the public by paying a realistic fee. An extremely lucid and useful document on this subject has been issued by the Museums Association (see 1.08) and should be read by every researcher not only for its information content but also for the opportunity it provides to look at picture research through the museum curator's eyes. The scale of fees recommended in the leaflet continues to be low by commercial standards, but is at least realistic.

Using public collections to maximum advantage

Like every category of picture source we shall be looking at, the public collections present a spectrum of advantages and drawbacks and only the individual researcher on an individual assignment can decide whether the balance is for or against.

The secret of using the public collections to maximum advantage is, first, knowing what they've got and, second, knowing how to get it from them. Planning and preparation will pay off in the long run, so the wise researcher will make it her business to familiarise herself with, and to keep a note of, the procedural arrangements of the major sources. Many of them issue leaflets giving guidance on how to use them, and detailing conditions and charges: file these for future reference for, though you may learn to master a particular system while you are actually using it, after you have used a few others you will start to forget it.

Remember that, though they are the biggest, this does not mean that the material in public collections is necessarily unique. Naturally places like the *Bibliothèque Nationale* will have material that nobody else has, but somebody else may have copied it. And though the *British Museum* has a fabulous wealth of prints and engravings, a relatively tiny collection like the *Mary Evans Picture Library* will have a few items that the *British Museum* does not have.

2.03 Commercial Sources

The fundamental difference between commercial sources and public collections is that the former normally receive no outside financial assistance. They are wholly dependent on the income they receive from making their material available for others to use.

Consequently they must charge an economic rate for their services, which will almost inevitably be higher than that charged by the public collections. The differential is not as great as it used to be; nevertheless you can still get a picture from, say, the *Wallace Collection* at a price which reflects only the material expense involved and none of the overheads of maintaining the collection or the service, let alone any question of profit which might be used for enlarging the collection or enhancing the service.

But it is precisely that word 'service' which indicates the other side of the coin. While the public sources are collections first, lending sources second, with the commercial collections it's the other way round. This does not mean that commercial sources are never worthwhile collections in their own right: many are private collections made accessible to the public by their owners as a means of raising funds for the enlargement of the collection. But all commercial sources have this in common, that they are primarily geared to providing a service for researchers, and this is true whether they take the form of a comprehensive photo agency, which handles its items like groceries in a supermarket, or a private collection of lovingly gathered specialist material, where the research operation is more like visiting someone's home than conducting a commercial transaction.

Historical collections

Only a few countries are fortunate enough to possess historical commercial collections: there are only about a dozen in the world, located in France, Germany, the United States and Britain. In addition there are a number of collections which are not specifically historical in scope but do include a certain amount of historical material.

The rates charged by historical collections are generally higher than those of public collections of comparable material, but lower than those of photo agencies with modern material. They combine some aspects of commercial sources with other aspects of public collections—briefly expressed, this means that they offer the high standards of service (and relatively high fees) of the commercial service, but at the same time feel a concern for the collection as a collection, as something more than a retrieval system. An historical archive will take pride, for instance, in filling its gaps, like finding a portrait of Dr Guillotin or a picture of Fonthill before the tower collapsed.

From the researcher's point of view, the biggest difference is likely to be one of accessibility. The commercial historical library will generally have been built up as a conscious and consistent process, filling gaps and extending scope as required, a way of working not usually practicable for a public collection, which is built up by accretion in the form of specific purchases or bequests, often with the condition that they be kept as independent collections. The commercial source, on the other hand, can integrate its material to form a unified and easily accessible whole. In particular, it is usual for commercial collections to be arranged by subject-matter, whereas in public collections, even where the material is not held in a number of separate collections, arrangement is as likely to be by artist or some other system more suited to the museum's needs than to the researcher's.

Commercial collections tend also to be more flexible than their public equivalents. Old engravings—originals—will be found side by side with copyprints, transparencies, and such diverse material as ephemera, music covers, posters, and so forth. It is this breadth of outlook which chiefly characterises the commercial source, together with the fact that it is likely to be continually adding to its material, filling gaps or developing stock not only for its own satisfaction but also in direct response to what researchers ask for. So, though commercial sources may not boast the treasures of the public collections, they may well be better suited to the researcher's needs.

Some historical collections, as a matter of principle, confine their material to items of which they possess the originals: in which case there is a good chance they will hold material which cannot be found elsewhere. Others will hold copyprints of material in public and other collections, perhaps on an agency basis: this is generally because they have been asked to photograph such items by clients. Now that the public collections are tending more and more to manage their own photographic and library functions, this type of secondhand source is tending to disappear.

Modern sources

General sources of modern material tend to be photo agencies, in which the work of many individual photographers is gathered together for convenience in more comprehensive collections. This type of source is discussed in the following section.

The remainder comprise a wide variety of more or less specialist collections. The following are some of the types of sources.

Specialist sources

These are often collections of material gathered by, say, an enthusiastic railway or underwater photographer. The material may reflect a strong personal interest, or be the result of some chance circumstance whereby an individual finds himself in possession of a collection of music sheets or whatever. Sometimes their material can be duplicated in larger collections, but they repay patronising because they generally bring a greater enthusiasm and more expert knowledge to their subject. What is more, knowing their field intimately, if they aren't able to provide what you want they can generally indicate who can: they will often join in your project with zest and prove invaluable allies. There is, of course, the likelihood that they will not be so well organised as a larger collection and lack some of the facilities, but such obstacles will not deter the adventurous researcher on the quest for fresh and hitherto undiscovered material.

Industrial firms and organisations

Most companies keep some kind of record of their activities, even if it is only photographs of their new factory wing: if the firm is a big and well-organised one like *Shell* or *Esso* the photo library will be extensive and well-organised. Material from such sources is often available free of charge, provided certain conditions are observed: naturally the material must not be used in any context which will reflect badly on the company, and due credit must be given.

It is worth bearing in mind that firms dealing in a particular commodity may well have pictures relating to it. *Stanley Gibbons*, the postage stamp people, maintain a comprehensive library of photographs of stamps. Auction rooms, like *Christie*'s and *Sotheby*'s, take many photographs for their catalogues, and these may be available to the researcher.

Learned societies and professional organisations

Most such societies have gathered together a small collection of visual material related to their interests, even if it is only a collection of portraits of past presidents. Such material is generally available at little or no cost, provided you can persuade them that what you are doing is in the best interests of their organisation. Although in the past such collections have not been geared to research, they are tending to become more aware of the need to make their material accessible: the *Royal Aeronautical Society*, *Nuffield College* at Oxford and the *Royal Photographic Society*, are all instances of the type of source which can be of value to the researcher.

Political and religious organisations

Trade unions, political parties and religious and missionary bodies often maintain picture files which, though intended primarily for internal use, can be made available to outsiders for purposes in sympathy with the aims of the organisation. The *United Society for the Propagation of the Gospel*, the *Zionist Archives* in Jerusalem and the *Trades Union Congress*, are examples of the institutions which can be used in this way.

Tourist organisations

Most countries maintain state-subsidised tourist boards to encourage tourism, often with offices in most major cities, and these are usually pleased to supply their photographs as a free service. Once again, it is important that the pictures are not used in any way that reflects badly on the country concerned, and they may well want to see the text or script before they grant permission for use.

The other shortcoming of such material is that it will tend to show the country in the most favourable light—the sun will be shining, faces will be smiling, there won't be a beggar or a slum in sight. But if all you're after is a nice picture of Buenos Aires, regardless of the state of Brazilian politics, this is a good type of source. The *British Tourist Authority*, the *National Trust* and local Chambers of Commerce are additional examples.

2.04 Agents and Press Agencies

The largest category of picture sources comprises the commercial photo agencies, in which the work of a number of photographers is gathered together and handled by an agent. Because many of them are specifically geared to the needs of newspapers and periodicals, they generally provide a fast and efficient service.

The most usual arrangement is that the photographer hands over his photographs to an agent—usually to only one in any country, on an exclusive basis. The agent takes care of all aspects of selling the photographer's work, and the resulting fee is split. Thus the photographer need waste no time in filing and paperwork, but is free to carry on up the Amazon or the Khyber doing what he's best at, knowing that his interests are being looked after back home. By and large it is an arrangement which suits all parties concerned: it makes most efficient use of the administrative set-up, and is certainly far more convenient, if less fun, for the researcher, who doesn't have to go trailing round each individual photographer hoping that he won't be away on an assignment at the time.

In the past it was probably true to say that a photo agency was only as good as the photographers whose work it handled. There were some which prided themselves on, and were respected for, their very high standards: such agencies accepted the work only of the world's finest photographers, and then only the very best of their work. These exacting standards were inevitably reflected in their fees.

Today there is a general levelling-up among photo agencies as the quality of work improves. In this heavily competitive field, no photographer or agency can survive unless he/it can offer high-quality material. So though there are still some agencies which have an outstanding reputation, they are no longer so sharply differentiated from the others as they once were.

Standards of service also play an important part. The agency which can not only offer good material but provide ease of access, rapid order processing and a high research capability will have an edge over its rivals.

The other variable is cost: here again the tendency is for rates to level out. *BAPLA*, to which most British agencies belong (see 1.07) has a recommended minimum rate. Probably the majority of agencies charge somewhat more than this minimum, but in general the differential is honestly reflected in the quality either of material or of service (see, for rates, 2.11).

Press agencies

Establishments such as *Associated Press, Central Press, Keystone*, etc., are deliberately geared to the needs of the newspaper, magazine and television world. In London they tend to be located in the Fleet Street area and retain the urgency and immediacy of their environment.

Their material is available very rapidly, if not instantly: facilities are streamlined, with in-house photographic departments for both colour and black-and-white material. Because time is the all-important factor, it is essential that the researcher should not waste their time. The requests you make should be precise and clear, specific not general, and with all the supplementary detail that could help to make it easier for them to find precisely what picture you need—e.g., the precise date of a specific event or the exact location of a scene.

The back files of such agencies contain much important historical material, and naturally each passing year adds to the historical interest of the older material. Until recently these agencies, preoccupied solely with the here-and-now, tended to take little interest in their back files. Today, with instant nostalgia the theme of so many publications, they are more aware of the value of their old material and are more ready to make it available to the researcher.

Press agencies are highly competitive. Only experience will teach you which source is most likely to give you a good picture of, say, the arrival of a pop star at London Airport or give the fullest coverage of a riot in Beirut. To a large extent there will be, if not duplication, then overlap, as all press agencies are linked to one or more of the international photo services which means that, within hours of an event occurring, syndicated pictures of it are available to all members of that syndicate throughout the world. Cases have occurred in which an agency has claimed a picture to be theirs only for it to be shown that it is an identical picture, taken at the same moment by a different photographer sitting at the first man's elbow.

A special arrangement exists with regard to photographs of British royalty. Since the royals are always news they run the risk of being followed everywhere and all the time by hordes of photographers. To avoid such harassment, and to avoid wasting photographers' time unduly, the major press agencies operate a pool system whereby they take it in turn to cover royal happenings, and the pictures are made available to all those who form the pool. So it hardly matters which agency you go to for your royal material; you will find more or less the same pictures at each one.

Colour stock libraries

There are many agencies which deal exclusively, or almost so, in colour transparencies, as these are required more and more by certain types of publisher. Colour transparencies are also easier to handle and stock than black-and-white material. In point of fact, as any honest photographer will tell you off the record, colour photography is actually easier than black-and-white: not only is the actual taking of the picture easier in normal circumstances, but processing is simplified because the film taken *is* the resulting transparency, and there are no intermediate processes of negative and print making.

Why, then, do picture sources charge twice as much for colour as for black-and-white? Partly because the basic material costs—the film and the processing—are much higher; and partly because the transparency, being an original, is unique. With a black-and-white photograph, if a print is lost or damaged, a new copyprint can always be made from the negative. Once a transparency is lost or damaged it is gone for ever. True, transparencies can be duplicated, but this involves a certain loss of quality, and is expensive.

In virtually every case, while you may or even must *purchase* black-and-white prints, you will be allowed only to *borrow* colour transparencies; furthermore, there will be a holding fee if you keep them beyond a certain period. Also, because transparencies are unique, the fee for loss or damage is very high—£200 is BAPLA's recommended minimum, and many libraries charge a great deal more than that, particularly if the material is irreplaceable; e.g., a photograph of an actual event (see 3.10).

The photographs which make up a colour stock library were often originally taken in connection with a specific assignment undertaken by the photographer. What you are being offered is either material which has already been used, or alternative photographs taken on the same assignment but not used. The agency should tell you which pictures have or have not been used previously if you are anxious to avoid using material which has appeared elsewhere. Sometimes the fee will be affected by whether or not the picture has been previously published.

General and specialist collections

Most photo agencies try to cover as wide a subject area as they can, but inevitably some tend to be stronger in one area, others in another. And there are some which limit themselves from the outset to certain fields of interest. Thus, while all press agencies will cover the highlights of the more important sporting events, such as Wimbledon or Wembley, comprehensive coverage of sport is available only from sources which set out to provide this. You can opt for the higher selectivity but limited choice of the general library or the bewildering profusion of the specialist, according to your needs. In the same way, you will need to create your own repertoire of preferred sources for such material as the following:

● Topical current events—such as the latest hijacking
● Portraits of people in the news and eminent living figures
● Background pictures of everyday life—landing fish at Grimsby, an Egyptian street market, opium smoking in Saigon

- Ethnographical subjects—initiation ceremonies in New Guinea, marriage customs in Lapland
- Topographical stock shots—the New York skyline, the Blue Mosque at Istanbul
- Wild life and natural history
- Reproductions of fine arts, paintings and artifacts
- The arts—theatre, ballet, rock concerts
- Sporting events
- Stock 'situation' pictures—families on the beach, children at school, girls with no clothes on.

For each of the categories listed there are one or two sources that are better than the rest: no one library will give you the best of all of them. Only experience will teach you which you prefer, and even if I were to recommend names you might not agree with me. Even technical quality is no sure guide: juvenile violence may be better expressed by a photo which is out of focus and tilted to one side than by a more 'perfect' picture which lacks immediacy.

You will take into account the quality of the service, too, the speed and efficiency with which they process your order, the helpfulness or otherwise of the staff. And always bear in mind that size is no criterion: a collection can be small simply because it has weeded out its poor material and contains only the best.

2.05   Private Sources

Because the realistic researcher concerns herself chiefly with the material she knows she can get at without too much trouble, she will tend to think mainly in terms of established collections such as those described in the preceding chapters. However, a good proportion remains in private hands. Some of it is inaccessible for the simple reason that the owner does not care to allow access, but more often it is the difficulty rather than the denial of access which is the obstacle. Though you may know, for example, that the finest portrait of Lady Jane Grey hangs, never photographed, on the wall of a moated castle on the West Coast of Ireland, but that a second-best is obtainable on transparency from an agency in central London, you will, unless your time and your budget are unlimited, opt for that second best. And few will blame you, least of all your editor who will not lightly put his hand into his pocket for the cost of getting you and your photographer to the painting's location. But you'll do well to keep always at the back of your mind the possibility of the option of a private source which could enable you to present fresh and hitherto unused material to your editor.

Most private material falls into one of two categories: the privately assembled collection, gathered by an enthusiast in specific subject, or the personal property of people who simply 'happen to have it' by reason of inheritance or some such circumstance. In either case, one thing is certain: they have the right to do what they like with their property, and you have no right to use it unless they grant you permission. So, if they allow you to use it, there is no question about who is doing who a favour, even though you end up by rewarding them financially for the privilege.

So, whether you are approaching a collector or an owner, you must try to put yourself in their shoes and use your tact to see the transaction from their point of view. Though most collectors are proud, openly or secretly, of their collections, they may be chary of having their extent revealed publicly, sometimes out of sheer competitive possessiveness, sometimes out of the reasonable fear that public exposure may tend to increase the value of such material and make further acquisition more difficult and more costly.

But, at the same time, most collectors like to have their collections appreciated, so if you show a genuine interest in what they have, you may well be able to flatter them into allowing you to reproduce it. But you may have to reassure them every inch of the way—that their treasures will be treated with care, protected against loss or damage and completely insured, that they will not be used in any way which implies disrespect either for the material or its owner, and so on. In short, try to imagine how you would feel if the item was yours, and then you're not likely to go far wrong.

No private collector will expect a researcher to know as much about his subject as he himself does, but he will cooperate more willingly with an informed inquirer who can ask intelligent questions. So do a bit of homework before you pay your visit: it's easy enough, generally, to get a book out of the library which will fill you in on the background of the subject. In the same way, if you wish to photograph a family portrait from a stately home, a few minutes spent on the family background will reassure the owner that you know what you are about.

Locating private sources

Most private material is unlisted in any directory. The more obvious collections are listed in the *Picture Researcher's Handbook*: some very

Dark Satanic Mills – or Palaces of Industry?
Above, from the *Oracle of Health* of 1835 and, *below*, from the *Illustrated London News* of 1851

Above, woodcut. Highwaymen on Hounslow Heath, 1729. From *The Newgate Calendar*

Below right, etching. Henrietta Maria, queen of Charles I (etched by Robert Walton)

obscure photograph collections can be found by browsing through the *Directory of British Photographic Collections. Museums and Galleries in Great Britain and Ireland* and *Historic Houses, Castles and Gardens* include a great many places where interesting material may be found, and the AA/Reader's Digest *Treasures of Britain* is another useful source book (see 1.08 for details of all these).

But of course the most rewarding ones will be those that aren't listed in any directory. How are they to be tracked down? One useful point to remember is that most collectors belong to a society dedicated to their subject—the Ephemera Society (see 1.07) is a notable example, but in fact there are societies reflecting virtually every field of interest. The secretary will generally be happy to act as liaison between you and a member if you can assure him your interest is serious.

Specialist periodicals are another source of information. Here, too, almost every field of interest has some kind of journal or newsletter for the exchange of information. UFO buffs have their *Flying Saucer Review*, numismatists have *Coins and Medals*, lovers of the pantomime have *Panto*! If you don't find the information you need in such journals, you can always advertise your needs.

For the most part, however, it remains true that such obscure sources have to be unearthed, one by one, by the diligent researcher. You hear on the grapevine of a man down in Somerset with a superb collection of old farm implements—make a note of him. You read a piece in the newspaper about a collector in Hampstead whose passion is black-and-white minstrels—note her name. You spot an acknowledgement in a book to a specialist in the history of powerboat racing—jot down the reference. Whatever it is, however far from your current inquiry, note it then and there in your files: you never know when it will be just what you need.

Today almost anything from the past—and these days the past comes right up to yesterday morning—is collected by somebody somewhere. The use of unconventional material gives the editor and designer a chance to vary the appearance of a book which might otherwise be visually monotonous—the title page of a book's first edition, a trades union banner, a tram ticket, a menu card, a family snap, the written side of a postcard, a page from an old newspaper, a song sheet, a postage stamp—all these can lend diversity to a page of text and give the eye a rest from more conventional items. And every one of them is being collected by someone, somewhere.

2.06 Criteria for Selecting Sources

In almost every instance, you will have a choice of picture sources from which to obtain your material. This is true even of many unique items, for some other source may have copied the original: for example, a photographer may have copied a medieval manuscript from a museum, and it makes sense to use his photograph rather than go to all the trouble of arranging to have it copied all over again, unless of course you are for some reason dissatisfied with the existing copy and reckon you could get it done better. Again, a particular engraving may be owned both by the *British Museum* and by the *Radio Times Hulton*: various factors will influence your decision as to which source to approach.

Faced with such a choice, your decision will be based on a balance of criteria, each of which may or may not be relevant to your current assignment. Among these criteria are:

- Range of material—the breadth of choice available, and its diversity—e.g., some sources will have only straightforward illustrations while others will complement them with ephemera, etc.
- Quality of material
- Ease of borrowing originals or obtaining copies
- Convenience of location and ease with which you can secure an appointment
- Convenience of access to material
- Speed of service—how long will you have to wait to obtain material after you have located it?
- Strictness or flexibility of conditions imposed by source; e.g., length of time material may be held
- Expertise of staff: if you are working on a complex or obscure theme—e.g., wildlife or technology—it is reassuring to know that there are experts who will save you from making wasteful errors
- Helpfulness of staff: no researcher can hope to turn up every item in an archive that could be relevant to her assignment, but sympathetic staff who take an interest in your needs will show you material you might not have found on your own
- Provision of back-up facilities, such as on-the-spot photostat machine, in-house copyprint facilities, access to reference books etc.
- Finally, and alas generally most important of all, cost.

Because every picture source is unique, it is dangerous to attempt generalisations. However, on the following table we try to show which type of source is likely to score best on the above headings. (Some, such as geographical location, do not of course lend themselves to such evaluation.)

	Public collection	General commercial	Specialist commercial	Private
Choice	**	***	**	
Quality	***	**	***	***
Ease of access	*	***	**	*
Speed	*	***	**	*
Expert staff	**	*	***	***
Personal interest	*	***	***	***
Back-up facilities	*	***	*	
Cost	***	*	**	***

(Note that, in the 'cost' item, the more stars, the *lower* the cost.)

Apart from the fact that they represent only the roughest of generalisations, the ratings shown above will be significant only in terms of a particular assignment. On a long-term television series speed will not be as crucial as on a transmission on a magazine programme. When you know precisely what you want, it doesn't much matter whether or not the staff are knowledgeable. And while cost is always a factor on every assignment, you must always remember that time, too, costs money: to obtain an expensive picture easily and quickly can actually save money as compared with getting it at a bargain price after days of hunting.

So, before tackling each assignment, you must get your priorities in perspective, and evaluate the available sources in terms of those priorities. Roughly speaking, it will work out like this:

● Where cost is all-important and time is not, a public collection should be your first choice
● Where time is more important than money, a commercial collection may save you money in the long run as well as enabling you to meet your deadlines
● Where precision and accuracy of the material is crucial, go for a specialist source if one exists
● If you have a theme but no specific requirements, look for a source which offers open access and encourages you to browse.

2.07 Procedure

Apart from knowing what sort of material a picture source holds, you need to know how it makes that material available. Considering that all picture sources have much the same problems to overcome, it is astonishing how varied are the solutions they have found. You will save yourself a lot of misunderstanding if you approach each unfamiliar source as if you have no idea how it works, for assuming it works one way only to find later that it works in another way can be time-wasting and even costly.

It is absolutely essential, before taking pictures from any source, to make sure you know their conditions. Many sources have these, or the more important ones, printed on the delivery note which comes with the pictures they send you: *read them.* Others have a printed leaflet listing their conditions: ask for a copy and read that, too.

Here are some of the questions for which you will need answers before you make use of a picture source.

Requests

Do they accept requests by 'phone? By letter? Do they allow, or actually insist on, personal visits? Do they *prefer* any of these methods?

Appointments

Do they require visitors to make an appointment ahead of time? If they do, what is the usual interval between the request and the appointment?

Authority

Do they require a written letter of authorisation from your employer?

Access

Do they permit direct access to their files, or must you wait while a staff researcher brings selected material to you? If the latter, and if the material they select is unsatisfactory, will you have to make a further appointment, or will they do additional research then and there?

Taking material away

Will they allow you to take away immediately the material you have selected? Or will you first have to clear permission for it? Or will you have to order copyprints? Or send in a photographer? Will you have to pay in advance?

Taking material on approval

Is there any limit to the number of items you may borrow?

Borrowing charges

Will there be a charge if you simply take away material on approval?

Other charges

Do they charge Service Fees, Holding Fees, Access Fees, etc.?

Restrictions and limitations

Is the use of their material restricted in any way—for instance, that it may not be used in advertisements, or must be used in its entirety?

Official forms

Do they require an official document to be completed before pictures are supplied?

All this sounds horribly complicated, though in practice in most cases there's a straightforward 'yes' or 'no' answer to each of those queries. The point is, *there is no such thing as 'normal' or 'standard' procedure.*

2.08 Retrieval Systems

The way pictures are filed within the picture source is out of the researcher's hands. All you can do is go along with the system, whatever it may be. Nevertheless, an understanding of the problems involved in filing, cataloguing and indexing pictures will help you to use resources more effectively, whether doing on-the-spot research or in formulating requests made by letter or phone.

All retrieval systems start with this paradox: *a picture is put into a file only that it may be taken out again.* The more thoughtfully it is filed, the more readily it will be retrieved. Conversely, an unintelligently filed picture can be to all intents and purposes a lost picture.

Until comparatively recently it was tacitly assumed that pictures could be filed and catalogued along the same lines as books. Only in the past few years, as the interest in visual documentation has increased so rapidly, has it become evident that picture collections possess characteristics and present problems different from those facing book librarians. The very creation of the Art Libraries Society (see 1.07) is an indication of the growing professionalism of the picture librarian as a separate species.

Some of the differences are obvious enough. Books are generally filed, to start with, in broad general categories—Art, Theatre, Travel, and so forth—with such subdivisions as may be called for. In this respect pictures present no new problem: they too can be filed broadly by subject, though with certain limitations we shall look at in a moment. But when it comes to filing within those general sections, difficulties emerge. A book can be catalogued by either title or author; but this isn't suitable for more than a very few types of picture. Fine art, yes, can be filed under Cruikshank, Rembrandt, Hockney. But the vast majority of pictures are not by 'name' artists, and their creator's names are matters of almost complete indifference. A photograph by Thurston Hopkins may be wanted *because* it's by Thurston Hopkins, but probably more often because it's a good picture of whatever it is.

As for titles, they are even less helpful. Apart from the fact that most pictures do not have formal titles, what would be the point of filing a Victorian engraving of a child with a dead pet under 'Early Sorrow' or a photograph of a country scene as 'A Rustic Idyll'?

Well, of course the inventors of library retrieval systems aren't so naïve as all that. The formal systems, like Dewey, are flexible enough, and possess a coherent framework capable of accommodating visual material in all its complexity. Unfortunately, 'complexity' is the *mot juste*. The systems are capable of doing the job: but are they the best way of doing it?

The human factor

The books in which the pictures will appear, the television and visual education programmes in which they will be shown, are aimed at *people*. They are selected for the impact they will make, the emotion they will convey, the information they will communicate. Only another human can choose, from a selection of illustrations, the one which will most effectively achieve that impact, emotion, information. That old cliché, that a picture is worth a thousand words, is a testimony to the fact that a picture does not simply convey a message, it does so in a unique way: while showing you a particular scene, it can communicate—instantly and often subconsciously—a whole emotional climate which will affect the way you feel about what you see.

No computer could select a picture of a street in Birkenhead which would evoke a given emotional reaction in the viewer: no formal system can subdivide such pictures under 'cheerful', 'depressing', 'nostalgic' or 'calculated to arouse indignation against the capitalist system'. So the pictures of Birkenhead's streets must be filed in such a way as to allow the researcher to make her own selection.

Well, that's obvious enough. But couldn't some kind of systematised retrieval system be used for all stages except that final one?

Again, yes, it certainly could: but a doubt remains as to whether it would be the most effective answer. For here another human factor emerges, the fact that, for almost all of us, our visual memory is far stronger than our verbal memory. How often do you hear people say 'I always forget names, but I never forget a face'? We may forget whether John Stuart Mill's book is titled *Liberty* or *On Liberty*, or whether *Discours sur la Méthode* was written by Pascal or Descartes (and anyway, do you list it by French or English title?), but we will have a vivid memory of a painting showing a Victorian family in a country house, the father giving his son a glass of wine despite his wife's disapproval, even though we don't recall—if we ever knew—that the title is 'The last day in the old home', the artist Robert Martineau, and its date 1862.

This is not to argue that a picture retrieval system must be based, or even rely, on human faculties. The primary elements, at least, must be computer-recognisable if there is to be any inter-library compatibility. But to seek to eliminate the need for human recognition is not simply to sacrifice commonsense to methodology, it is to reduce the practical effectiveness of the system. Picture research, like all top-quality merchandise, must be 'hand-finished'.

Demand classification

In practice, all picture sources recognise these realities, whatever lip-service they may pay to systematised methods. Most operate on *ad hoc* principles, using a pragmatic approach which, for want of a better label, may be termed *Demand Classification*. In other words, the pictures are arranged in the way that is most convenient for the people who have to locate them.

The guiding principle of demand classification is this: *the mental path trodden by the person who files a picture should anticipate that likely to be taken by the researcher seeking that picture.* Like a detective reconstructing a murderer's movements, the filer should be able to say to herself: 'If I were looking for this picture where would I expect to find it?' And, hey presto, one mental process should match the other!

Nothing is ever that simple, of course, and so, behind the filer, there must be the formal structure to fall back on, or at least a system of cross-indexing to guide the researcher back from the wrong path to the right one so that, if looking for pancake-tossing on Shrove Tuesday and lost in Religion or even Food and Drink, a signpost is there to lead her safely to Customs.

So once the researcher has been given the basic breakdown— People here, Places there—she should, by using commonsense and with a few signposts, judiciously placed, be able to find her way round the files unaided by staff.

The overall lay-out

The starting point of the classification system is the overall lay-out, and there are several schools of thought about this: the two basic alternatives are alphabetical or by subject.

Alphabetical

The sections are arranged as their heading dictates—Accidents followed by Advertising, Animals, and so on. The great merit of this system is its simplicity. The great defect is that different users will use different terms: will you find Mrs Pankhurst under Suffragettes or Women's Rights, or simply Portraits?

Subject

This has the merit that related fields can be located adjacently—Museums next to Exhibitions, Cooking alongside Eating. But it is even more dependent on the human element. Just because one person thinks of Drugs as a subsection of Crime doesn't mean that others will feel the same way. Certainly a basic breakdown into PEOPLE, PLACES and THINGS is a good start: views and portraits can be separated out without much difficulty, though there are small points, such as does Archaeology go with Topography, and do people's Birthplaces go with their Portraits or in the appropriate Places? Another not-too-awkward separation will remove Historical Events, even if you have then to decide whether subjects like

Emigration and Exploration are incorporated or not: and were the exploits of King Arthur fact or fiction?

Difficulties really start when you come to Things. One general library in London divides them as follows: Transport and Travel; Industry and Commerce; Sport and Entertainment; Nature; Behaviour; Daily Life. But you can see that this is a fairly arbitrary separation and can lead to many ambiguities—do Street Scenes belong in Daily Life or Transport; if Hunting is a sport when enjoyed by the Quorn or Pytchley, what about when it is hunting by the Navaho Indians or the Barotse tribe?

Clearly it is unrealistic to aim at perfection in this matter: all one can hope to achieve is a system that works well enough most of the time. Given a reasonable degree of commonsense, either the alphabetical or the subject system will work reasonably well, as you will discover if you visit the *Mansell Collection* on the one hand or the *Mary Evans Picture Library* on the other.

But there are other problems:

Size

Picture libraries share with book libraries the problem of what to do about items which ought to be housed together but are of such disparate size that this is impracticable. But, whereas all but a few elephantine books can be put on a shelf which need not be too far from the shelves where the smaller books are housed, large pictures have to be stored in a quite different way from small pictures. Many museums and print collections have great portfolios which contain poster-size pictures next to ones the size of a postcard. This may be acceptable for a museum collection, but it isn't for a working library, particularly one granting open access to outsiders.

So the general practice is to house large-format pictures separately: small-format (say, up to 25 x 20cm) are generally housed vertically, in filing cabinets, mounted on stiff card or in suspended files; larger items are filed flat, less accessibly but more protectively.

Ephemera

Many libraries possess a certain amount of one-off material —showcards, brochures, programmes, cards, catalogues, etc.— which simply can't be filed along with the pictures. This usually necessitates separate boxes, box files or drawers.

Rare and valuable items

There is, understandably, a growing reluctance to allow the rarer items to be handled casually by researchers, and this can form another class of material which is separated from the main files, usually in display albums or portfolios.

Books

Most picture libraries have a supplementary collection of books containing additional visual material—runs of illustrated periodicals, for example. Ideally these will be indexed and cross-referenced in a manner which is compatible with the arrangement of the library's primary material, but they still constitute another separate element.

Transparencies and slides

Where colour material is in the form of transparencies and slides, it is usually impracticable to house it with prints and photographs. In a source with a large quantity of both colour and black-and-white material this is likely to involve what amounts to a complete parallel system.

Each of these problem categories involves the physical separation of material which ought to be related as closely as possible. The library should do all it can to minimise the effects of the separation by placing related material as nearby as possible and by generous use of cross-referencing. It is also desirable that, as far as possible, the system by which the disparate material is filed should be the same as that adopted for the primary material.

Cross-referencing

The picture librarian is continually faced with the need to decide into which category should be placed a picture which is relevant to more than one section—e.g., a picture showing gipsies telling fortunes with cards at a race meeting. Here the picture could be filed under Racial Types/Gipsies, Occult, Games and Sporting Events, not to mention the artist's name.

The only practicable answer is to file the picture under one of the headings, and place references to it in the other files. Ideally, of course, additional copies of the picture will be made and filed under each of those headings, which is one way to make a picture library seem four times as big as it really is.

Captioning

All kinds of additional difficulties crop up with the business of captioning. Should Firenze be filed as Firenze or Florence in an English-speaking collection? There was once another Italian city named Nizza: in return for dubious favours received, the Italians gave it to the French who rechristened it Nice: what is a historical library to do which has pictures of the city before *and* after the handover? Tschaikowski, Chaykovsky, Tchehov, Chekhov—the choice is yours. The *Dictionary of National Biography* lists all its titled subjects under their family names—would you think of looking for the Duke of Marlborough under Churchill, Castlereagh under Stewart? (luckily, the book is cross-indexed!) Most libraries who favour the demand classification system file Robert Stewart, Viscount Castlereagh under C, because it was under that name that most of his career was accomplished: but they try to remember that he ultimately succeeded to the title of Marquess of Londonderry, and put a reference card in to remind themselves. They are unhappy if they have to be inconsistent when it comes to Lord Beaconsfield, whom they like to file as Disraeli, and the Earl of Orford, better known as Robert Walpole, whereas John Spencer-Churchill is clearly recognised most easily as the Duke of Marlborough . . . Here again, if one is to remain sane one must not aim at perfection. In the end it comes down to commonsense, both on the caption-writer's part and on the researcher's. You must be prepared to find the great fair of Nijni-Novgorod under Places in one library, Fairs in another: children working in factories under Social Conditions here, Industry there. Commonsense will take you nine-tenths of the way; after that you'll have to ask a native.

2.09 Conditions

No picture source will allow its material to be used unless the client has, either openly or tacitly, accepted its conditions. *It is essential that you should be aware of these conditions before you obtain pictures, as the use of pictures is taken as implying that you accept the supplier's conditions, whether or not you have read and formally accepted them.*

Most sources have printed lists of conditions and will be glad to let you have a copy. Often these conditions, or the more important of them, are printed on the Delivery Note which is supplied along with the pictures: sometimes the more immediately relevant of them are printed on the reverse of the picture itself.

The majority of British commercial sources subscribe to the list of conditions recommended by *BAPLA* (see 1.07). These comprise a long and legally-phrased document, designed to safeguard both parties in the event of dispute. Some picture sources will provide a simplified list. Many sources will have individual conditions of their own to cover their individual circumstances: for example the *National Portrait Gallery*, naturally concerned that the pictures in its possession should not be poorly reproduced and so reflect badly on the gallery, stipulates that any transparencies made of its material should be a minimum of 13 × 13cm in size. Likewise, the *Tate Gallery* requires that the minimum transparency should be 5 × 4 inches, and moreover that 'the paint area of a picture, or the area within the outline of a sculpture, must not be masked out, cut down, superimposed with type matter, or in any way defaced'.

Broadly speaking, the list of conditions you will be required to accept, or will be deemed to have accepted if you use the pictures, will cover the following aspects of picture borrowing. All these subjects are of course discussed in other parts of this guide, and we indicate the appropriate sections:

- On what terms are pictures supplied? On approval, outright purchase, etc? (3.06)
- Who is held responsible for pictures while borrowed and until returned, and for ultimate payment? (3.09)
- How long may borrowed pictures be retained without payment? (2.10, 3.09)
- What credit line is required? (3.12)
- What service fees, holding fees, etc., are charged? (2.10)
- When is payment due? (3.11)
- Who is liable for loss or damage? (3.10)
- What are the stipulations regarding voucher copies? (3.12)
- Who is responsible for copyright, model release, etc.? (2.12)
- Are there any restrictions regarding on-loaning of material or sending it abroad? (3.09)
- Are there any restrictions on the way material may be used—e.g., not for publicity, only whole picture, etc.? (2.01)

If a condition is unacceptable

It may happen that for some reason you cannot go along with all the conditions. For instance, it may be essential to your assignment that material is forwarded to another country. If so, you should raise the matter at the first opportunity. Most picture sources are prepared to be flexible in such matters, and to make exceptions by special agreement. But, if so, be sure to get permission in writing in case of later argument.

2.10 Fees

In the simplest type of picture-finding operation, you find the picture you want, its owner gives you permission to use it, and that's all there is to it. But it is not often quite that simple. More frequently the owner will expect to be paid for making the picture available; sources will expect to be indemnified for their service even though the picture is not ultimately used, or if the picture is kept beyond an agreed period, or for many other contingencies. You should therefore be prepared for any of the following charges:

Fees for using the picture

Reproduction Fee

This is a simple payment in return for permission to use the picture. It is usually granted for one use only (one illustration reproduced once in one edition of one publication in one language in one specified area). The amount charged may be a simple flat rate for all contingencies, but is more likely to vary according to the rights you require and the type of use you make of it. (See 2.11 for Rates and 3.11 for Rights.) The reproduction fee is the main source of income for most picture sources, and the main expense for your client.

Copyright Fee

The copyright holder on any picture which is still in copyright (see 2.12) has the right to charge a fee for the use of his picture, whether or not you obtain the actual artwork (see Glossary, p 199) from him.

If the copyright holder also supplies the artwork (e.g., if a photographer lets you use one of his photographs) then his reproduction fee will generally incorporate his copyright fee. This is generally true, too, of commercial photo agencies and the vast majority of commercial sources. But if you want to use a picture from a book—for example, one of Arthur Rackham's illustrations—you must obtain permission from the publisher or copyright holder, and will probably be expected to pay them a copyright fee. So in such a case you will have to pay two fees—one to, say, *Mary Evans Picture Library* for letting you use their transparency of the picture, and another to the Rackham estate for their copyright.

It is very important to keep clear in your mind this distinction between the reproduction fee and the copyright fee, as they are frequently confused by people who should know better. You may find it helpful to think of the copyright fee as giving you permission to use the picture *in principle*, the reproduction fee as giving you permission to use it *in practice*.

Fees for services in connection with making the picture available to you

Access (or Facility or Disturbance) Fee

This is charged by sources such as museums, in the event of your wishing to photograph an object or picture in their possession. It may be additional to a copyright fee or incorporate it. What you are doing is paying for the facilities provided by the physical owners or custodians—staff time, use of lighting, moving the object, and general 'nuisance'.

Service, Search or Research Fee

Under various names, this is a fee charged by a picture source to cover the costs incurred in making the picture available to you. Sometimes these costs include the task of retrieving the picture from the files, and, in the case of a larger order, where the staff may have to retrieve many pictures from many different files, you can understand that they may have to do a good deal of work on your behalf. The fee also covers the cost of handling and paperwork—checking the pictures out and back again when you return them, invoicing, postage, packing, and any normal wear and tear on the picture, its mount or other container.

Service fees are not always charged on small, simple orders, particularly from a regular client, though it is becoming more and more the rule to charge a service fee on every order where no pictures are ultimately used. It is almost invariably charged on large orders or where special trouble has been gone to. Because practice varies from one picture source to another, you should be prepared to find a service fee charged on:

● every order, whether or not any pictures are ultimately used
● every order, but deducted in whole or in part from the reproduction fee if pictures are ultimately used

- any order where no pictures are ultimately used
- any order where only a small proportion of pictures is used
- any order on which the picture source has been put to particular trouble.

Rates for service fees vary as widely as the circumstances in which they are applied. In 1978 *BAPLA* was recommending a minimum service fee of £10 on every order, whether or not any were used, so presumably most photo agencies were charging more or less this sum. *Popperfoto* charged £5, but only if no pictures were used. *Radio Times Hulton* charged £4 and *Mary Evans Picture Library* £5 under similar circumstances.

Although it might seem desirable for practice to become more standardised, in practice a rigid structure could well work to the researcher's disadvantage, for then a standard fee would have to be charged big enough to cover all eventualities, regardless of individual circumstances. As things are, the service fee is charged on an *ad hoc* basis, taking into account various factors which are not easy to assess objectively.

It is important to bear in mind that sources charge service fees not as an additional source of revenue, but simply to cover costs: without them, many orders would result in actual financial loss to the source if no pictures were eventually used, so that their cost would have to be subsidised by the jobs which *did* materialise.

In practice, service fees are not usually very high, and are in any case subject to negotiation. Nevertheless, it is very important for the researcher, when doing business for the first time with a source, to establish what is their practice regarding service fees.

Interim Service Fee

This is similar to the service fee, but is charged on jobs where initial work has been carried out, and the picture source involved in some expense, but where there is some delay or no immediate prospect of publication. In such a case, the source asks the client to pay an interim fee to cover the costs incurred to date. It is usually modest.

Print Fee

Strictly speaking, this is not a fee as such, but a simple material payment for a copyprint, transparency or other item of artwork commissioned or purchased by the client. In most cases it is a standard charge, little if anything above the standard fee charged by the photographer or artist. It may, of course, include the cost of taking the photograph as well if the picture has not been copied before and when it is not the source's custom to bear such costs itself (see 3.07).

Print fees are charged by virtually every source which supplies copyprints or duplicate transparencies on a non-return basis. The rare exceptions are certain commercial firms, tourist organisations and the like, where providing pictures is part of their promotional function and, though they like their pictures back, they don't mind unduly if they don't get them, and are prepared to write off the cost.

Some picture sources have their own photographic departments, in which case print fees are generally lower than those charged by sources who have to depend on normal commercial suppliers.

Fees incurred under certain circumstances

Holding Fee

If you borrow pictures, as opposed to purchasing copyprints, you will almost certainly be liable to a holding fee if you keep them longer than a specified time and do not eventually use them. Typically, the period is one calendar month, but this does vary so be sure to ask when you borrow pictures.

Holding fees are not usually very high, but you should be aware of how quickly they can mount up. Thus at the *Mary Evans Picture Library*, whose holding fees are probably the lowest charged anywhere, they charge 10p (or 20p for colour) per picture per week after the first (free) month. This sounds modest enough until you work out that if you keep a batch of twenty pictures for four months over the allotted period, you will be liable for a bill of £26. If they were to charge the recommended BAPLA rate of £1.50 per week, the same job would cost you £390 in Holding Fees alone. The ASMP recommendation in the USA is $1 a day for transparencies, $1 a week for black-and-white.

Some sources call this a blocking fee, and this term does convey the primary reason for charging such a fee: as long as you hold the picture, you are blocking its use by some other client and so depriving the picture source of potential revenue. It is true, you may argue, that they may have other copies, but it costs money to copy a picture.

It is important to remember that holding and blocking fees are charged not as an additional source of income but to discourage clients from hanging on to pictures for longer than they need. In practice, many sources will waive the holding fee or extend the period if you ask their permission and explain the reasons for your request.

Copper engraving. James II (anonymous)

Mezzotint. Charles I (engraved by Faber after Van Dyck)

Nor, in most cases (but not all), are such fees applied to pictures which are being used.

Remember that sources like to be told about what's going on at your end: having let you borrow their pictures, they like to be kept informed of progress. So long as you recognise this, they will generally be ready, on request, to adjust their procedure to meet your circumstances. But read carefully the conditions printed on your delivery note, and if you hand the pictures over to some other member of your organisation, be sure that they in their turn fully understand the conditions attached and undertake responsibility for returning the pictures within the Holding Period, or contacting the source before it expires.

Hire Charge

This is really a variant of the holding fee. A few sources which loan material charge a loan fee from the start, simply for borrowing the picture and irrespective of eventual use. Thus the *Tate Gallery* charges £15 for borrowing a transparency for up to 3 months, and £10 a month thereafter, though if it is returned unused within seven days no charge is made. The *National Portrait Gallery* charges £8 a month for the same service. These high hire charges are balanced by low, often nominal, reproduction fees.

2.11 Reproduction Rates

Your employers will naturally expect you to find them the best possible pictures at the lowest possible price.

In most fields it is probably true that the best pictures are the most expensive. A 'name' photographer will naturally charge more than a young unknown. The astute researcher will watch out for the young unknown whose pictures are as good as the 'name' photographer's, and whose rates are lower. But, alas, it won't be long before his name too becomes well known—perhaps as a result of the researcher's efforts—and his fees rise. There is also the fact that 'names' help to sell the book.

It would be contrary to British law if all picture sources were to gang together and charge the same rates. As it happens there isn't the slightest chance of this happening. Those which have top-quality material would rather sell fewer pictures for higher prices: others will compete by charging less and hoping to do a bigger volume of business in consequence. *BAPLA; CPNA; IIP* and other bodies (see 1.07) recommend *minimum* rates to which their members nominally subscribe.

Reproduction rates vary substantially and by playing the field the canny researcher can often pick up 'bargains', going to one source for one type of material, another for another. She can even spot a picture in Source A and reject it knowing she can get it cheaper from Source B. But at the same time she will also learn that price is by no means the only yardstick when it comes to deciding which picture source to patronise.

What you are paying for

A piece of colour film costs a few pence. To process it costs a few pence more. Yet you will pay between £20 and £100, sometimes even more, to use a colour picture. Robbery?

An old copper engraving can be picked up in a street market for £2 or so. Yet you are asked to pay £10 or more simply to borrow and copy it. Extortion?

Well, you must bear in mind that the colour film may have on it a picture of the summit of Mount Kilimanjaro on one of the few days in the year when it is not shrouded in cloud, and for which the photographer had to wait—and wait—then seize his chance, hire a land-rover or a helicopter, lay on a guide, and dash to take his picture before the clouds regathered . . . And you must bear in mind that the library which has the insolence to ask you to pay £10 to copy its £2 picture asks no more to lend you a plate from Diderot's *Encyclopedia* (current saleroom price £6,000+) or a print finally run to earth in the *Marché aux Puces* after years of searching . . .

The point is, when you pay a reproduction fee you are not paying for the material cost of a picture, you are paying for the cost of making that picture available. You are paying for its housing in a collection—for the mounting, identifying, captioning and copying, for the heating and humidity control to keep it in good condition, for the filing, cataloguing, indexing and cross-indexing, for its handling, packing and posting, for the delivery note which accompanies it and the invoice which follows it and the 'phone call asking what you've done with it, for the staff who helped you find it and who told you where to go for the pictures they couldn't help you with, who gave you a mug of coffee to sustain you and whose loo you used and whose reference books you consulted and whose 'phone you borrowed and whose brains you picked.

Above all you're paying for the finding of the picture in the first place—for someone to be in the right place at the right moment with a loaded camera ready to take the unique photo of Prince Charles not quite falling off his horse; or for unearthing, in an obscure bookstore in the Weissadlerstrasse in Frankfurt, a scrap album of German film stars of the 1930s when Dietrich wasn't even a mother and Anton Walbrook was named Adolf Wohlbrück . . .

The cost of service

Most reproduction rates genuinely reflect what it costs that particular picture source to make its material available to you. Why, then, the often considerable differences between one source's rates and another's?

● The cost of obtaining the pictures in the first place. A picture source which prides itself on the high quality of its material will pay more for a 'name' photographer or for rare prints and books.
● The cost of keeping the collection up to date. Some types of material grow out of date. If you want to be sure of finding a picture of Singapore as it is this year, not as it was four years ago, you must be prepared to pay more to a source which invests in replacing its material. The same can be true even of historical collections: some make an effort to fill gaps while others make do with what they already possess. Again, you must be prepared to pay more to a source which is trying to meet your needs.
● The cost of providing a better service. Some sources try to give prompter service; their material may be more thoroughly indexed; they may employ more qualified staff.
● Some sources are financially self-supporting while others are in effect subsidised (see 2.02 and 2.03). This is likely to be reflected in the services and facilities they provide.

Rates cards

Most picture sources issue a rates card of some kind. You should obtain copies of rates cards issued by all the sources you use; by comparing them you will find it easier to decide which source to use, or at least which one you should start with.

Bear in mind that rates cards are periodically—often annually—revised. You cannot expect a picture source to send its new card to everyone who might use it, nor can you hold them to their old rates just because you didn't know they'd introduced new ones. It's *your* responsibility to check, every time you use a source, what their current rates are.

Rates structures

Rates structures vary from the simple to the complex. At one extreme is an establishment like the *National Portrait Gallery*, which has a basic charge (1978) of £4.25 black-and-white, £15 colour for English language, double for world rights (plus the hire fee already referred to in 2.10). At the other extreme are the French photographic agencies, most of which subscribe to a standard fee structure, involving page after page of complex tables, which takes into account almost every conceivable factor and contingency.

It is attractive to aim for a simple rates structure, but in practice this is apt to be unfair. An elaborate structure is more flexible and enables the source to distinguish between—for example—a cookery book aimed at 20 million housewives and a study of fans aimed at perhaps 1,000 collectors, a travel guide intended to be sold round the world and a guide to bridle-paths in West Somerset. It would be unfair to ask *The Rabbit Fancier's Weekly* to pay the same rate as the *Reader's Digest*.

Rates for printed publications

Rates structures for books and periodicals are generally based on one or more of the following criteria:

● How big is the area of the printed picture?
● How widely will the publication be distributed?
● How many copies will be printed?

Among major British commercial sources, there are some whose rate structure is based on print area; some on market size; some on print area and market size combined; and some on print run, print area and market size combined.

Besides these basic yardsticks, there are several additional factors which, though not insisted on by every source, are widely observed. The examples I quote are all from current rates cards and are selected because they are characteristic, but they are not necessarily applicable to other sources and any of those mentioned may have changed by now.

Colour

More is invariably charged for pictures reproduced in colour. *BAPLA* recommends an overall +100% rate, and this is followed by the majority of sources, though some—*Ann Ronan* is one—have a lower increase of +75%. *Popperfoto* charge +100% at the lower price levels, but diminish the rate till it is down to about +40% at the higher levels. The *Mansell Collection* distinguishes between reproduction from prints and from transparencies: for prints they charge +100%, for transparencies they have a separate structure which at low levels works out at some +500% over their black-and-white rate. The *Radio Times Hulton* also has a separate structure. Such examples make it plain that a source that is cheap for black-and-white isn't necessarily so for colour, and vice versa.

When colour pictures are reproduced in black and white, the colour rate is reduced by 25% by some, by 50% by others.

Dummies and other promotional uses

Typically 50% the normal rate.

Covers, jackets

Front, usually +100%, back +50%. When a picture is used as a wrap-round, both front and back, this could be +150% but is often less.

Frontispiece, endpapers

From +50% to +100%

Reference or artist's copy (see Part 5 for definitions)

This is frequently an awkward area. To the client it may seem invidious to pay a large sum for a print which the artist and designer simply use as a guide for their own artwork. To the picture source, it is just as much work supplying a picture for reference as for reproduction. Consequently, this kind of rate is generally negotiable: typically, a picture supplied for reference or artist's copy only is charged at 50% the normal reproduction rate, but there may be a minimum fee of £5–£10.

Other editions

Basic rates are for reproduction in one edition in one country only. Usual practice is to charge an additional 50% for any other edition, whether it is a subsequent edition for the same market, a simultaneous softback edition, a coedition or whatever. But this is a very complex area, for publishing practice varies widely and it is not always easy for the picture source to understand exactly what the publisher's intentions are, with the result that it is probably in this area more than in any other that misunderstandings occur with regard to rates. It is therefore essential for the researcher, playing her go-between rôle, to be clear in her own mind what the publishing plan is, and to spell this out in clear terms to the picture source, so that a fair rate can be agreed without acrimony.

Place of origin

A researcher may find herself researching in, say, England for a book which will ultimately be published in, say, the USA. While on the face of it it shouldn't matter to the picture source where publication takes place, in practice it is generally recognised that, in view of the great disparity in size between the US and UK markets, US publishers should pay more for the pictures they use.

Additional rights

Whether the structure is based on market or on print run, there will always be the possibility that the publisher will change his mind—perhaps to extend the print run, perhaps to produce a further edition. For this reason, many publishers prefer to make an outright deal with the picture source in the first place, purchasing unlimited world rights; this may cost them more initially, but frees them from subsequent complications. It also often gets them a favourable all-in price as the picture source, too, is glad to settle for a lower inclusive price which will save any further invoicing and paperwork.

Where this is not done, it is the publisher's responsibility—and therefore often the researcher's—to see that the picture source is informed that additional rights will be required.

Negotiating a discount

Most picture sources are ready to reduce their rates if given good cause. You can usually expect to command sympathy if you are working on behalf of a new publisher or a magazine not yet established; if you are producing something for a genuine charity; if the publication is aimed at a very restricted or specialist market; if it is a genuine non-profit undertaking. But you will lose the sympathy and the respect of your source if you try to obtain a reduction which is not really justified. After all, their costs are the same whether the picture is being used for *OXFAM* or *Vogue*.

Quantity, on the other hand, is another matter. Almost any picture source will do a deal if you use a number of their pictures, since this means less paperwork per picture for them; to lend out 100 pictures at one time is not nearly so laborious as lending out one picture a hundred times.

Quantity is a relative term. It can be as low as five, if you're talking about five front covers of a periodical, or pictures for an advertising campaign. For illustrations in a book ten is a more probable minimum, and many sources would not regard 'quantity' as signifying less than twenty. If you expect to use a good number of pictures from one particular source in a publication, it is generally advisable to negotiate a specific contract with them. This is especially the case with a long-term or multi-volume publication, such as a partwork or an encyclopedia. Publishers who specialise in this type of publication habitually draw up contracts for each new project with those picture sources they expect to do continuing business with.

Periodicals

Reproduction fees charged to periodicals, newspapers, magazines, etc., are generally at their own standard 'space rates'. The most notable exception is for special items such as a picture 'scoop'—a new official portrait of the Queen, for example—when you should reckon to pay an above-average rate.

As the phrase implies, space rates are calculated from the space occupied by the reproduced illustration, reckoned in column-centimetres for newspapers and some periodicals, square centimetres or fractions of a whole page for others. Special positions, such as front and back covers and other favoured spaces, may be taken into account. Rates are usually related fairly closely to circulation figures, but prestige publications will often offer lower rates, thinking—not without justification—that picture sources prefer to see their work reproduced in *Country Life* than in the *Gasfitter's Gazette*.

Most picture sources are ready to accept clients' space rates, though this may not be true of those who handle the big-name photographers. It is therefore important for the researcher to check that space rates are acceptable.

Where the publication has no space rates of its own, the picture source will generally make provision on its rates card for various grades of publication:

- newspapers, national
              local or provincial
- periodicals, national
              trade or technical
- house journals
- specialist or professional journals
- other media with restricted circulation.

Advertising

The rates referred to above apply only to the editorial content of a periodical. Use in advertising—and this includes any periodical which exists entirely for the sake of promotion—is generally negotiated for each individual assignment. So many factors are involved:

● type of media—posters, press advertisements, display material, packaging, etc.
● size of poster or advertisement
● number of publications in which an advertisement will appear
● number of insertions in any one publication, or number of poster sites.

BAPLA recommendations (1978) started at £70 for one colour picture used for one insertion in one publication: some rates cards give basic guidelines for advertising charges, but it usually ends up as a negotiated figure.

Television

Television rates are usually standard, set by the television company, and these rates are generally accepted by picture sources. A distinction is drawn between network transmission (throughout the country, though not necessarily simultaneously) and local or originating areas only (e.g., a programme designed by Granada for transmission only in North-West England).

Rates are based on the number of times, or the length of time, the picture is exposed: the technical term is 'flash'. Rates are normally expressed for 'first flash' with additions for 'repeat flashes' which may be:

● a second flash of the same picture in the same programme
● in a second transmission of the same programme at another time or in another country

World rights and unlimited rights may be sold, and this is often preferred when the programme is likely to be shown throughout the world. The broadcasting companies themselves are so well geared to the complexities of monitoring programmes and apportioning fees that they are rarely flummoxed by such complicated situations as arise when a programme is first shown, and perhaps repeated, in one country, and then sold to overseas markets.

Television rates are usually specified as 'non-theatrical': that is, an additional fee is expected if the transmission is shown elsewhere than on television, for instance in a cinema, theatre or exhibition hall.

Here is a typical television rates structure, taken from the rates card of one British source, to give an idea of the contingencies they expect:

- First flash, UK or any one country except USA
  Network
  Local or originating area only
  World
- First flash, USA
  Network
  Local or originating area only
  World
- Repeats
  Repeat flash in same programme
  Repeat transmission in same or other country
  Unlimited, including all repeats

2.12 Copyright

It is the researcher's responsibility to check and, where necessary, clear the copyright on every illustration.

Unfortunately copyright is a very complicated subject, with some areas still not wholly clarified, and those that are legally provided for full of traps into which the unwary may fall. The terminology is used loosely and often incorrectly, so there is often doubt whether you and your opposite number are talking about the same thing.

Fortunately, when you obtain pictures from established picture sources they will generally be well informed as to the copyright situation at least as regards the material they themselves hold. But, while in principle you can get by without reading the pages which follow, to have at least a general idea of copyright will help you to avoid some very expensive pitfalls.

(Note: The notes which follow apply, except where indicated, only to Britain. In practice they apply to most other countries too, but there are significant differences in the law between one country and another. If you obtain material from abroad, your supplier should be aware of the copyright position. If in doubt, check.)

'Copyright' and 'reproduction right'

Every picture is protected by two rights: *copyright* and *reproduction right*. Because they generally go together, the two are often confused. But the distinction can be an important one and, hair-splitting as it may at first seem, it is important that you understand the difference. *Copyright* is an abstract right in the picture as a created artifact, and applies both to the original picture and to any copies of it which may be made. Copyright belongs to the legal copyright holder (defined later) *no matter who owns the original or any copies of it. Reproduction right* is the here-and-now right to reproduce the picture, or a copy of the picture, and applies to the actual sheet of paper or canvas or photographic print or transparency. Reproduction right belongs to whoever legally owns that picture or copy. If several people own copies of the same picture, each of them owns the reproduction right in their copy of the picture, but none has any rights over the other copies, and it may well be that none of them also owns the copyright.

Except for pictures out of copyright (defined later) all pictures are covered by both these rights, and you must be sure you have secured *both* rights before you reproduce a picture in any way. In everyday practice, reproduction rights as granted by an established picture source will generally incorporate a one-time release of copyright for the purpose of that particular use but don't assume this to be the case without checking.

'In copyright' and 'out of copyright'

Every picture is either 'in copyright' or 'out of copyright'. This is chiefly a matter of its age—see 'duration' below. A picture which is *out of copyright* may in principle be used by anyone *once the reproduction rights have been cleared.* For this reason, out-of-copyright pictures are often said to be 'in the public domain'. If you personally buy a picture which is out of copyright, such as a 100-year-old engraving, the reproduction right is automatically yours and so you have the right to use it any way you like.

When a picture is *in copyright* then you must establish the copyright situation. In practice the owner of the picture will often either own the copyright also, or will have come to some agreement with the copyright-holder. But this is something you must check when you borrow a picture. Some sources—the National Portrait Gallery, for instance, who do not necessarily own the copyright in all the pictures in their possession—require you to obtain written authority from the copyright holder or his agent before they in their turn will give you the reproduction right in that picture.

It is extremely important to establish the copyright situation on every picture you borrow, because anyone who uses a picture without obtaining copyright clearance may become liable to pay a very heavy fee. The copyright holder has the right to charge whatever sum he likes; and, though most copyright holders are reasonable in their demands, they do not take kindly to infringement of their rights: when their pictures are used without permission first being sought they may demand heavy fees which the user has no option but to pay.

Duration of copyright

In Britain, a picture is in copyright for 50 years from the end of the year in which the artist or photographer dies. The artist need not be the holder of the copyright: he may have passed it on to his heirs, assigned it to a friend or simply sold it on the open market. (He could even have sold the copyright while retaining the picture itself.)

In the case of a work commissioned for a book or a periodical, the copyright is normally held by the publisher. If this is the case, copyright expires 50 years after the end of the year in which the picture was published.

This means that in practice most historical material—almost anything published before 1900 and much that was published before 1928—is likely to be out of copyright. (But again, remember that this does not mean that you are free to reproduce it unless you have also obtained the reproduction right; there is no expiry date for reproduction rights.) Bear in mind, by the way, that some people live longer than you might expect. Picasso may have done some of his paintings while Queen Victoria was on the English throne, but they will not be out of copyright until the 1st of January 2024!

The duration of copyright varies from one country to another. For example, copyright in France lasts for 64 years, in Germany (West)—70 years, in Holland—50 years, in Spain—70 years, and in the USA—56 years (28, renewable for a further 28). In the United States the copyright position is somewhat different than it is elsewhere. Copyright is not granted automatically, but has to be applied for and registered by the copyright holder, and renewed again after 28 years. If this is not done within a specified period, the material reverts to the public domain. The consequence of this sensible arrangement is that the copyright position on any given item is much easier to establish and the risk of confusion much reduced.

Tracing the copyright holder

You should always make every reasonable effort to trace the copyright holder. If the source from which you obtain the picture can't help, you will then try to find the artist or the photographer, if known; or, if the picture has appeared in a book or periodical and there is no picture credit (see 3.12), the publisher concerned.

If you don't know the artist's name or can't trace him, and the publisher went out of business years ago and nobody seems to have taken over his business, you may find yourself with no way of tracing the copyright holder. Your best course now is, first, to make every reasonable effort to obtain the information; then, second, to go ahead and use the picture. A good plan is to place an advertisement in a suitable newspaper or magazine, asking for the copyright holder to contact you. You will very likely get no reply, but, should the copyright holder turn up later and demand a fee, the fact that you can produce evidence of having tried to trace him will be an indication of your honest intentions, and you will be less likely to be clobbered. But if you follow this course of action you must always take into account the fact that the copyright holder has a legal right, any time within six years after you reproduce his picture, to demand his copyright fee.

A further precaution is to insert some such paragraph as the following in the publication containing the picture:

> *The publishers have endeavoured to trace the copyright holders of all pictures and photographs in the publication. If we have unwittingly infringed copyright, we sincerely apologise, and will be pleased, on being satisfied as to the owner's title, to pay an appropriate fee as if we had been able to obtain prior permission.*

Copyright of commissioned photographs

The most complicated area in the whole matter of copyright is one which frequently concerns the researcher, so it is very important that you understand it clearly.

The copyright of a commissioned photograph belongs to whoever commissions that photograph. In the case of a book or a magazine, this is usually the publisher (but sometimes the author).

But—and this is where the complications set in—even though the publisher commissions the photograph, and pays all the costs, he doesn't necessarily, or even usually, acquire the negative. The photographer retains it, so that, if the publisher requires any further prints from it, he will have to come to the photographer for the business.

If the photographer chooses, he may sell the negative to the person who commissions it, or the publisher may make it a condition of the commission that he is also purchasing the negative, in which case he may expect to pay the photographer a somewhat higher fee.

However, though the photographer retains the negative, he has no rights in the photograph, neither copyright nor reproduction right. He may not use it himself (except in a very limited way for personal purposes), nor may he make it available to anyone else.

The publisher, having commissioned the photograph, holds the copyright in it and can make whatever use of it he likes. He also has the right (if for instance he quarrels with the photographer or the latter disappears) to get another photographer to re-photograph the first photographer's prints, thus creating a second negative, which becomes the second photographer's property, and we start all over again . . .

In the case of photographs such as colour transparencies or pola-roids, where there is normally no negative, the situation is simpler. They become the property of the person who commissions them, and all rights go with them.

Copyright of non-commissioned photographs

When a photographer takes a photograph on his own initiative, the copyright situation is the same as for a work of art: the photographer retains the copyright and can dispose of it to others. If he allows one of his photographs to be used in a publication, he is selling only the one-time reproduction right: the publisher does not thereby acquire the copyright, and may not use it a second time without obtaining further permission.

Duration of photograph copyright

This is basically the same as for other types of illustration, but in Britain there are some additional complications brought about by recent changes in legislation.

When the photographer is known and holds the copyright in his picture, he or his assignees hold that right for the customary 50-year period from the end of the year in which he dies. If, on the other hand, the photograph was commissioned, and the copyright is held by, say, a publisher, there is a further complication:

● *Photographs taken before 1 June 1957* Copyright expires 50 years after the end of the year in which the photograph was taken.
● *Photographs taken on or after 1 June 1957* Copyright expires 50 years after the end of the year in which the picture was first *published*. This means that if a photograph is not published until many years after it was first taken, it still has 50 years of copyright to run from that *later* date.

Copyright of works of art

The copyright of any work of art remains with the artist, even if someone purchases that work of art, unless:

● the artist formally assigns the copyright to someone else, or
● it is a portrait (see below).

If you buy a painting, you may sell it or mutilate it or even destroy it completely, but you may not reproduce it yourself or give permission for others to do so without first obtaining permission of the copyright holder (assuming it is still in copyright).

Copyright of portraits

In Britain, portraits are subject to separate legislation if they are commissioned for money or other payment. In such a case, the person who commissions the portrait—not necessarily the sitter— holds the copyright. Even so, the duration of the copyright is still linked to the life of the *artist*, even though he has no rights in it whatever.

Copyright of copies of in-copyright works of art

When a modern painting is photographed, an additional dimension is added, so that, before you use a transparency of, say, Picasso's 'Guernica', you must clear:

● the artist's estate's copyright in the original
● the photographer's copyright in the photographic copy
● the owner of the transparency's reproduction right

In practice, chances are that whoever lends you the transparency will be legally empowered to grant you copyright clearance both on the original and on the transparency—but *you must make sure*!

Copyright of copies of out-of-copyright works of art

If you have commissioned a photograph of an out-of-copyright work of art—say, a painting by Gainsborough—and if the permission to photograph was given to you by the picture's owners with no strings attached (e.g., no limitation as to use once only, etc.) you can in principle do what you like with it, since the only copyright which now exists is your copyright in the photograph you commissioned.

You could in theory use it to advertise soap powder and there is nothing the original owners could legally do to stop you.

In practice, though not legally bound to do so, you would do well to observe a *courtesy copyright* (I am indebted to Julia Brown for this useful phrase) and ask the owners for permission each time you use it, and be prepared to pay a small 'courtesy fee' or send a free copy of the book in which the picture is used. Besides showing consideration, this can help to create a good relationship with owners you might want to approach again.

Use of copyright material for reference or artist's drawing

Copyright applies even though a picture is not used for direct reproduction but for reference only, *so long as the original picture is recognisable in the new artwork, in part or in whole.* This applies even when only a detail is used, or when a re-drawing is made by an artist—for instance, when a photograph is converted into a drawing for a school textbook in the interests of simplicity, or style, or simple reproductive quality.

Reference fees are usually only half the reproduction fees. It is much safer to pay them than to try to get away with not paying any fee at all, for any infringement is likely to be heavily penalised and such practices have been the subject of several legal battles.

Geographical limitations of copyright laws

A country's copyright laws relate only to publication in that country. They do not apply to material located and/or created in that country but used in other countries. For example, the noted French painter Jean-Yves Quivala died in 1927. So his paintings are out of copyright in England, where the copyright-duration is 50 years, and can be used freely (subject to reproduction rights) in a book published in England (and in any other country where the duration is 50 years, of course). But Quivala is still in copyright in France, where the duration is 64 years, so if a French edition of the book is contemplated, copyright clearance must first be obtained from the French copyright holders.

I have done my best to set out the subject, as it affects the picture researcher, in simple and non-technical terms, but these notes must not be taken as giving a proper legal account. While I believe that if you follow their guidance you will be in little danger of causing legal offence, they do represent a gross simplification of the legal provisions, and I can take no responsibility for the consequences of any actions based upon them.

2.13 Making the Most of Visiting A Picture Source

If you send a written request to a picture source for a picture of Isadora Duncan, and they send you one, all you will have learned about that picture source is that they are a reasonable place to go to for pictures of Isadora Duncan, how long they take to process orders, and how much they charge.

If, on the other hand, you pay them a visit, you will not only make sure of obtaining the most suitable of their pictures of Isadora Duncan, but you may learn many other things about them which may stand you in good stead in the future.

Wider choice

If you do your own research at the source, you will almost certainly see a wider selection of material on a given subject than they would have sent you through the post, no matter how conscientiously the staff researchers do their job. In the end, it is only you who can know which picture would be the most suitable. What is more, if you discuss your quest with the staff, they may make further suggestions which they would not have done in response to your original request.

Notes for the future

While hunting for Isadora, you are sure to catch at least a fleeting glimpse of their other material. You may even, after fulfilling your request, ask if you may browse through other files, just to familiarise yourself with the sort of material they have. This will give you a much firmer idea of what sort of material to request from them in the future.

Personal contact

If it's that kind of library, you may be able to make friendly contact with one of the members of the staff, who will get some idea of the kind of material you prefer and enable her to deal more effectively with orders you send her in the future. This will pay off when you're in a rush and can't spare time for a personal visit. You will also be able to pick her brains and ask advice in the future, even when not making a specific inquiry.

Copper and steel. Fountains Abbey, *above*, on copper in 1770 and, *below*, on steel in 1866

Right, woodblock from a
drawing by George Cruikshank

Below, halftone. When printed
at the proper size, these dots are
invisible to the naked eye.
Actress Phyllis Dare in *The
Tatler*, 1904

The 'feel' of the collection

Every picture source has its own ambiance which is dictated less by the nature of their material than by the way it goes about the job of making it available. Two libraries dealing in almost exactly the same kind of material can be as different as chalk and cheese. Only a personal visit can enable you to sense this character and make your own response to it, deciding whether or not it's 'your kind of place'. Once you do, you will find yourself able to use that source more effectively, and you will find them more willing to give you good service, readier to put themselves out for you.

Not all picture sources encourage, or even allow, visits: and not all those which permit visits also allow open access to their files. Over and above these factual differences, there will be intangibles—places that make you feel welcome and others that don't; some where you feel at home from the start, others where you can't get out soon enough. After your visit, you may decide you never want to set foot in there again, but that is something you won't know until you've paid them at least one visit.

In time you will build up a list of sources which you use for 'remote' requests—a straight simple photo of Winston Churchill, perhaps—and others you'll visit when a good long browse is most likely to give you a wide coverage of, say, child life in the eighteenth century.

If they are not too busy, most librarians are delighted to talk about the place they work and the material in their collections. They may even take you on a conducted tour—after all, it's as much in their interest as yours that you should be well informed about their resources. So though you go to visit them to get your Isadora Duncan photo, you may come away with a mental note that, should you ever need them, they're pretty good for music hall posters and Hollywood stars of the 'thirties. Nearly all picture sources have a certain number of 'treasures' which for one reason or another—value, size or simply because they don't mix in with the rest of the collection—are separately housed and whose existence you would not ordinarily suspect. Only in the course of a personal visit are you likely to learn of their existence.

Don't forget, too, that picture librarians don't only know about their own collections; they can often tell you about other collections you've never heard of, or give you useful tips about ones you don't know well.

Asking questions

Here are some of the questions you might ask when visiting a picture
source:

● Do they think of themselves as particularly strong in any respect?
  And, if you can manage to phrase it tactfully, do they have any
  shortcomings, areas in which they don't hold material, to save you
  bothering them in future?
● Do they have any special collections?
● Do they have foreign as well as British material?
● Do they act as agents for any other source—handle material from
  foreign museums, for instance, or from a learned society or pro-
  fessional body? Do they have a tie-up with an overseas source so
  that you can order the latter's material through them?
● Do they have back-up facilities, such as runs of illustrated period-
  icals?
● Do they have a stock of ephemera as well as straightforward pic-
  tures?
● Do they have historical as well as modern material, or vice versa?
● Are they continually adding to their stock?
● Do they publish a catalogue or any other printed information
  about themselves such as a rates card?

PART THREE

THE ASSIGNMENT

3.01 Taking on an Assignment

Not all researchers will be working on 'an assignment', and, of those who are, not all will be burdened with the entire responsibility from initial briefing through to publication. Though in this third part we cover every phase of a comprehensive operation, you will certainly find that only parts of it are appropriate to your needs.

Research for book publishers has been chosen as the pattern, because this type of work involves the greatest complexity. Those working for television companies, weekly magazines, exhibition designers or advertising agencies will find that their work is less complex—though not necessarily any easier—than that described here.

It should go without saying that no researcher should take on an assignment without being fully aware of what she's letting herself in for. But it is very easy to forget to ask some of the crucial questions. If you are a staff researcher, many of these matters will be taken care of for you, but if you are a freelance you should, before accepting an assignment, be sure you know the answers to the following.

What is the subject of the assignment?

Most researchers should be able to tackle any research assignment, even if the subject is unfamiliar: tempting though it is to do yet another book on a subject you know well, to explore new territory is stimulating and broadens your experience. However, if the subject is highly specialised you may simply lack the background knowledge necessary to do a good job, in which case it is best to refuse it at the outset rather than risk damaging your reputation by doing an unsatisfactory job.

How much time is being allowed?

If you think the time is insufficient given the size and complexity of the assignment, *now* is the time to say so. Publishers work to tight schedules which have to fit in with printers' dates and other factors, and they must be able to rely absolutely on your producing the pictures on time. If you don't think their timetable is a realistic one, tell them now so that they can perhaps readjust it, or assign you an assistant.

Where and how does your client expect the research to be carried out ?

Is it a book which is best researched on the spot, because it deals with a specific region, or because the best material on the subject is housed in a particular location?

Does your client want the pictures themselves in the first place?

The client may prefer verbal indications or photostats, the actual pictures to be ordered when he is ready to go to press.

In the case of long-term projects, publishers are often unwilling to incur too much expense at the outset, so it may be that all your client will need is the assurance that the pictures exist and can be obtained at short notice. In which case all you will supply is a list of references, indicating locations and any relevant numbers or titles, perhaps accompanied by a set of photostats (see 3.08). This will make your job simpler in the short run, though it will not necessarily save you very much time as it is the locating not the obtaining of the pictures which will consume most of your time.

Is a sufficient budget being allowed?

As we shall see in 3.04, budgeting is a complex and delicate matter: but your experience will tell you whether or not the client is being realistic. If you think he hasn't a hope of obtaining the pictures he wants at the price he is prepared to pay, now is the time to tell him so. If he is not willing to re-think, back out of the assignment straight away: it can only lead to disaster if you take on an assignment knowing that the budget is inadequate.

Will you be provided with a specific picture list?

Whether you are given a list or whether you will compile your own list from the author's text, or the editor's summary, or simply from conversation with the author or editor, can make a very great difference to the time the assignment takes, and you must be sure your client appreciates this. But there are two sides to the matter. While it is true that making your own picture list from a text or from briefing is time-consuming, at the same time it gives you the chance to draw on your own experience to get pictures which you know to be readily obtainable: whereas, if you are given a specific and detailed list, you may find you have to go to a lot of trouble to track down a particular picture your author has a vague memory of having seen in some not very confidently identified book (see 3.02).

If a freelance, will you be working from home?

Will office space and facilities be made available to you by your client? Can material be sent to you at his office? Can you make use of his telephone and telex facilities?

Who is responsible for storing the pictures, and for possible loss or damage?
(See 3.09 & 3.10.)

Who will negotiate fees?

Who will be responsible for returning pictures?
(See 3.09.)

Given what you know from the answers to the foregoing, is adequate remuneration being offered?
(See 3.05.)

As the cross-references show, these matters are dealt with in greater detail in the sections which follow. But it cannot be emphasised too strongly that any doubtful items should be sorted out at the start, before you are committed to the assignment. A good assignment depends on mutual trust and understanding between client and researcher, and a client who is unwilling to listen to your doubts is not a client worth working for.

3.02 Planning the Research Programme

On some assignments you may be asked to find only one or two pictures; if on the other hand you are collecting material for a heavily illustrated book, you may be looking for dozens and even hundreds of pictures. In this chapter we assume a sizeable assignment, though most of what is said would be true of any job.

Your starting point may be any one of the following:

● author's own picture list

- editor's picture list
- author's manuscript or completed text, perhaps in galley-proof form
- author's or editor's synopsis

If the author knows his subject well, he may indicate the features in his text which require illustration. He may even be able to tell you precisely what pictures he wants, perhaps enclosing photostats. Much will depend on how familiar the author is with the problems of publication. There is a danger that he will simply give you a list of pictures he has seen in other publications. If adhered to, this is a limitation on the researcher, whose job is reduced to hunting out those publications and tracing where the pictures were originally obtained from. But, apart from your own dissatisfaction, there is the more important danger that the book itself will suffer by such lack of originality. If you feel this to be the case, have a word with your editor, especially if you have sufficient knowledge of the subject to feel confident that you can find replacements which will be as effective and more original.

However, an author's list which specifies the precise illustrations is generally the case only with specialist books where particular illustrations are needed, or where his text makes specific reference to individual pictures. More often, what you will get on your picture list, whether from the author or the editor, is a list of more general requirements, such as 'Marie Antoinette in youth or just married'. Ideally, the requirement will be precise enough for you to know just what you're looking for, but not so precise that you have no freedom of choice.

Questions to ask

When making up your own picture list, you will need to ask the following questions:

- How many pictures are wanted?
- All black and white? All colour? Or in what proportion?
- Must colour transparencies be of any particular size? (See 4.04.)
- What method of printing will be used? (See 4.07.)
- What budget is available? (See 3.04.)
- Where historical pictures are required, must they be strictly contemporary or will a 'reconstruction' from a later period be acceptable? (See 4.02.)
- What type of reader is the book aimed at?

The answer to this final question will guide all your picture selection. You will choose quite different pictures for a textbook intended for secondary schools than you would for a book on the same subject aimed at an older readership. A book intended for the popular market will be illustrated differently from a scholarly publication. In some types of book a good appearance is an important element as it will help sales, so in a popular book on French architecture you might tend to include attractive pictures of Loire chateaux surrounded by early morning mist and half-hidden by autumn leaves, whereas for a scholarly book on the same subject you would go for pictures which brought out specific architectural qualities.

If the book is one of a series, your editor will show you other books in that series, and that will give you a good idea what kind of pictures are wanted. Looking at other books brought out by the same publisher can be helpful: a book on the French Revolution published by Weidenfeld & Nicolson, for example, will use somewhat different pictures than a book on the same subject brought out by Cambridge University Press—not necessarily better or worse, just different.

Before compiling your own list, a visit to a library is valuable to have a look at other books on the subject: an hour or two spent in this way can save days of work later. You will not necessarily get any specific indications of pictures, but you will get a general idea of the pictures others have used to illustrate the subject, which may or may not be the best available. You may see specific pictures which you can use, particularly if the book is not a recent one: you will also see some that you should avoid, perhaps because they have appeared on the jacket of another book. In some fields, repetition is unavoidable. It would, for instance, be quixotic to try to depict daily life in eighteenth-century London without using any pictures by Hogarth.

When you do come across a picture you think you could use, note its original source. Modern books are punctilious about picture credits (see 3.12), but this is a comparatively recent innovation: few books published before 1950 bothered to indicate where the pictures came from. If the library has a photostat machine, take stats of possible pictures.

Note all available information, for there may be several different ways of obtaining the picture you need: you may get it from the original source, or from the publisher who used it, or from the photographer employed by the publisher to copy it at the original source.

Your working list

By combining your own experience with such indications as those described above, together with any help the author and editor may have given, you are now in a position to make up your own list, which may be an amended version of one you were given, or one you have built up for yourself.

Every picture researcher will have her own way of laying out a picture list: the format suggested here is only one of several.

Lay out the list in three columns:

● The items themselves, with essential information—e.g., in the case of a little known personality, his life-dates; in the case of a historical event, its precise date; etc.
● Notes on the type of picture wanted, name of artist or photographer, etc.
● Possible sources

Thus a picture list for a history of France might contain such entries as these:

Marie Antoinette as young girl	Portrait by Levallois COLOUR	Louvre Cooper Bridgeman? Giraudon?
Battle of Camperdown (1 Aug 1794)	Loutherbourg (b & w) engraving	British Museum Mansell? Mary Evans?
Napoleon cartoon	Gillray cartoon, see Smith's *Works of G.* page 562	Macdonald? Mich. Holford? Radio Times?
Acre	COLOUR PHOTO	Rob. Harding? Ronald Sheridan?

A specific portrait of Marie Antoinette, which hangs in the Louvre, is indicated: you will probably not need to approach the Louvre itself, however, as it may have been copied by an agency specialising in fine art—perhaps Cooper-Bridgeman in London or Giraudon in Paris—and it will be easier to try them first. Similarly with the Camperdown picture: a historical archive like Mansell or Mary Evans is fairly likely to have the same item as the British Museum. The Gillray item has been published in a book: you can choose between approaching the publisher, the photographer credited with copying it, or a commercial library which may hold a copy. Only if these fail would you go to the less accessible original source and have it photographed. The modern colour photo of Acre is the simplest item, giving you a choice of many colour libraries specialising in topographical transparencies, of which Harding and Sheridan are just two.

Diversifying your sources

There is something to be said for getting a large number of pictures from a single source when this is possible. First, it can save you time, and, if you take a substantial number of pictures from a source, they will very likely give you a reduction in reproduction fees (see 2.11). However, there are dangers in putting too many eggs in one basket. By patronising one source from which you have obtained adequate pictures, you may be tempted not to bother visiting others and so miss the really marvellous material *they* have. There is also the danger that your editor may suspect you of skimping your work!

There is an additional factor, which is that it pays you to patronise as many sources as possible. It's true that not all sources are equally valuable but almost every one has something unique to offer, and by spreading your patronage you are helping to build up relationships with the greatest possible number of sources and so laying up good will for the future. If a picture source sees the final publication, and notices in it a lot of material which they could have supplied, but which you obtained elsewhere, they will be less likely to help you next time than if you had given them a fair share of the business. Obviously, every source, being only human, would like to have the lion's share of the business, but in the long run it pays everyone to distribute the business as widely as possible.

3.03 The Long-term Project

Certain types of project take years rather than weeks to complete—encyclopedias, partworks and other large-scale books, and also television 'epics' which must be planned years in advance. The accumulation of visual material for such assignments presents obvious difficulties.

Ideally, it's advantageous to start collecting the material from the start, building up as the project takes shape. But purchase of material which may or may not be used is a costly business—and it is notorious that in projects of this kind there are liable to be changes in direction or editorial policy which would completely change ideas about the type of visual material required. But if you don't buy the material, you have to borrow it—and no picture source likes to lend out large quantities of material for months and years on end. What are the other alternatives?

You can order copyprints or duplicate transparencies of all material

When you are pretty certain you will use a particular item, this is undoubtedly the best way. No holding fees will be incurred, you have the item securely in your files and won't have to make a second approach to the source. On the other hand, copyprints cost money, and on a large-scale project this can mount up.

You can make verbal notes

This has the advantage that it costs nothing besides your time. But the shortcomings are obvious, and the risk of confusion, as you attempt to reconstruct in your mind a picture that you saw many months previously, is apt to be frustrating. A further danger is that for some reason or another the material may not be available when you return to the source to exchange your notes for the real thing: they may have got lost in the interval, or been lent to some other client. For black-and-white items, which the source has on neg, this isn't a serious risk, especially if you've made a note of the reference number, but for colour it is more important.

You can make photostats of all the items you think could be useful

This is probably the most satisfactory method. Most sources permit you to make photostats of their material, at a cost of about 10p apiece, so long as they think there is a fair chance that you will come back to them for the originals. At this price, you can afford to take away a visual reminder not only of pictures you are fairly sure you will eventually use, but even of more doubtful ones. It also means that you can take a copy of material in books, which, if you decide you want to use, you can ask the source to photograph at a later date.

Unfortunately, you can't generally make photostats of transparencies. These must either be copied, or verbal notes taken, unless you are willing to incur the purchase price or holding fee involved. Inevitably, therefore, when collecting material for a long-term project you are going to end up with a file containing some originals, some stats, and some verbal notes.

The importance of keeping all this disparate material under tight control is obvious: the more care you take in the early stages, the more thankful you will be when the time comes to order the actual material for the book. And remember, there is always the possibility that for one reason or another you will not be the person who has to do that ordering; you may be transferred or fired, or get married or fall ill—a lot can happen in a year or two! So be sure to leave your notes in a form which can be taken over and readily understood by someone else.

Where they exist, make a note of all print or negative numbers, so that ordering can be done without a return visit to the picture files. If you have taken photostats, you can send them to the source and ask them to supply matching originals. With a visual memorandum there is no danger of confusion.

When completion date approaches, your preliminary work will be put to the test. The project which seemed to have all the time in the world a year or two ago has now become a high-pressure eleventh-hour tension-fraught business, and you will be grateful for everything you did in those early weeks to make your present life easier.

Ideally you should now be able to go back to each of your sources with a list of requirements, including photostats of some material and reference numbers for others. In some cases you will be ordering copyprints, in others borrowing transparencies and other material. Even at this late stage it is likely that some of the material may need to be held for longer than the source's stipulated holding period, so be sure to obtain the necessary clearance. Most sources are glad enough to extend their holding period if there is a strong possibility that the material will ultimately be used, but they *do* expect permission to be obtained beforehand rather than in retrospect. Once again, keep detailed notes of what material is obtained: besides documenting each item against your own list, it is a wise precaution to make a separate note for each source, listing all the material you have obtained from them and reminding yourself of permission to extend the holding period, agreed rates and any other relevant information. This will save you a good deal of time and anguish when doing the final job of informing each source which of their material has been used, and will also help you to return it promptly and efficiently.

Budgeting for long-term projects

In any long-term project, when it is likely that a fair amount of material will be obtained from a particular source over an extended period, it is usual to agree a fee per item at the outset, by written contract, both to make your budgeting simpler and to save renegotiation. It is usually possible to obtain favourable terms compared with standard rates. It is also usually possible to get the source to agree a price in line with what they are charging at the outset of the project, to apply to all material obtained for this project even though, by the time the work goes to press, their rates may have increased.

3.04 Budgeting

Unfortunately, unless you are exceptionally lucky in your employer, the question of money looms large in a picture researcher's life. A publisher will pay his printer, his paper supplier and his binder considerably more than he will pay his author, who creates the book in the first place, or his picture supplier, whose illustrations not only complement the text but also do so much to persuade the public to purchase the book and so enable him to pay his printer, his paper supplier and his binder and make a little something for himself.

The situation is indeed starting to change a little, but there are still too many publishers around who regard illustrations as a regrettable addition, to be taken into account only when the book is otherwise complete, and on which a minimum of money should be spent. With some honourable exceptions, British publishers tend to be much more blinkered in this respect than their opposite numbers on the continent of Europe: it is still comparatively rare to find a publisher's editor who has a really balanced and realistic concept of the relative importance, and therefore of the viable cost, of providing a book with illustrations.

Normal practice is to allocate a sum of money for the illustrations in a book taken as a whole. This sum is based on past experience, and the editor should have taken into account the fact that some pictures cost more than others—that colour costs more than black-and-white, that modern photographs cost more than old engravings, that big-name photographers charge more than their lesser known colleagues, and so on. He should also have taken into account that costs are continually rising, and should therefore add an appropriate percentage to what he paid a year or two previously.

There are two main elements in the picture budget, leaving aside for the moment expenses and print fees:

● The cost of conducting the research
● The fees paid to the owners of the illustrations and/or the copyright

If staff researchers are employed, the cost of research will simply be part of the publisher's overheads. It will be up to the individual publisher whether he allocates a certain number of man-hours to each book, or simply draws on the team as required.

The cost of using freelance researchers is considered in more detail in 3.05. At this point it is enough to note that the editor must allow for that cost over and above whatever other fees he has to pay. In this section we are concerned only with the budget for reproduction and associated fees.

When you take on an assignment, be sure you understand what the budget is expected to cover. Perhaps the most important factor is that of what rights are required. If a book is to be sold on the world market, reproduction fees will be double or more the basic rate, and your budget should be calculated accordingly. You must ensure, too, that there is sufficient margin to cover holding fees, unless they are to be counted as an extra; the same goes for any other expenses over and above the reproduction fees.

When doing a large production for an established publisher, the editor will generally have worked out a figure which you will then pass on to your sources: 'We are prepared to pay so much: will this be acceptable?' This makes life simpler all round and, if the figure has been realistically assessed, most sources will be ready to accept the suggested figure; but it limits the flexibility of the research programme in that you will thenceforth be tied to those sources which have agreed to accept the rate.

More generally it is up to the researcher to allocate the budget, and to negotiate each price, juggling high-cost items against low-cost ones to avoid overstepping the total. Eventually, of course, you will have to justify your decisions to your editor, but so long as he gets the pictures he wants at the price stipulated, he will be happy to leave it to you how you manage it. The wise editor learns that the more he pays his researcher, the more she is likely to save him by getting better value for his money.

The obvious way to start is by working out a rough average. If you have been allowed £1000 to illustrate a book in which 100 pictures are to be used, that is an average of £10 per picture. Since BAPLA's recommended minimum rates start at £11 for black-and-white (1978 rate) this means that, even if only one-country rights are required, you will have to find some pictures at less than £10 simply to meet your average. And that doesn't take into account the likelihood that there will be some pictures, perhaps ones essential to your list, for which you will have to pay more than the BAPLA minimum. If you want to include any colour, that sends the cost up dramatically, and if you need a colour illustration for the jacket you will have to pay a minimum of £25 and probably very much more, unless you can find a low-cost source for it. And low-cost sources don't usually have the kind of pictures which make for striking book jackets!

Free sources

Some sources will let you use their pictures free of charge and, if you are on a tight budget, one of your first thoughts will be how many such pictures you can use. These will be illustrations held by commercial firms, professional bodies or tourist organisations, subsidised collections which for one reason or another *want* you to use their pictures.

Of course there's a catch—though not necessarily a big one: you will be under an obligation not to use the picture in any way which will reflect badly on the lender.

Another likelihood is that these pictures will have been used elsewhere; and may in any case not be of very high quality, having been taken by a staff photographer. So, though a clever researcher may build up a certain proportion of her assignment with such material, it must be used with discretion.

Cheap sources

Despite BAPLA and other trends towards standard price levels, it is still true that some sources are noticeably cheaper than others. The public archives and museums, for instance, are generally cheaper than the commercial sources (though beware of 'concealed' costs such as transparency loan fees which can mount surprisingly high!). If you can afford the time, you will endeavour to obtain what you can from such sources, but this necessitates careful planning at the outset of the assignment in case the National Library of Argentina doesn't send you your prints in time to meet your deadline.

Asking for reductions

Most picture sources will lend a sympathetic ear to genuine hard-luck stories, but they have heard most of them before and are apt to be somewhat cynical when asked to reduce their rates because the book is intended for educational or charitable uses. Don't be surprised if they come back at you with the query as to whether your paper supplier and your printer are also reducing their prices? Remember, it is just as much work for the source to provide a picture for a non-profit project as for any other; there is really no reason why they should subsidise *your* philanthropy.

Naturally you want to obtain the lowest price, but most picture sources operate at a very low profit level and it is unfair for you to put pressure on them unless your own need is a genuine one. If a picture source feels that it is being exploited, this will create bad feeling, and

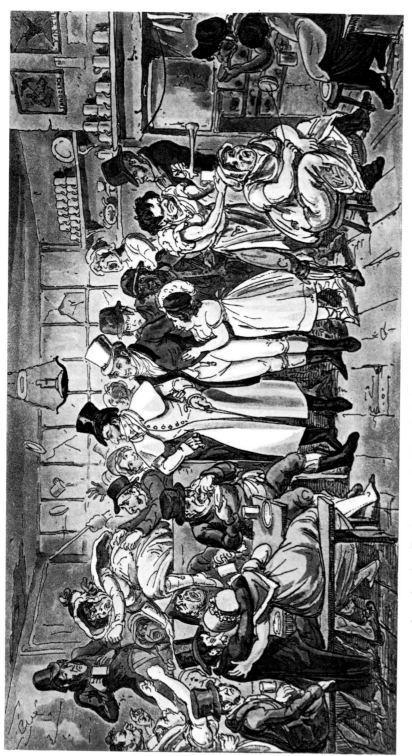

Aquatint. A coffee shop near the Olympic (coloured original by George Cruikshank from *Life in London*, 1820)

Lithograph. The French actor Chollet, by Alexandre Lacanchie

you, as the representative of your firm, will be the one to suffer.

On the other hand, asking for a reduction for quantity is another matter, for in this case you will be saving the source time and trouble, since it's little more work supplying twenty pictures than two. So there is something to be said, despite what we have said earlier about spreading your business as widely as possible, for obtaining substantial quantities of material from a single source if by so doing you can obtain a more favourable rate. By this means a source which would normally be considered 'expensive' can compete favourably with those considered 'cheap' and you stand the chance of obtaining better-quality material as a consequence.

When authors pay for illustrations

It was formerly normal practice for authors to be expected to pay their own illustration costs. This dated from the period when illustrations were regarded as an unnecessary luxury. Even though they might help sell the book and so benefit the publisher more than anyone else, they were regarded as an indulgence on the author's part and he had to find the money for them out of his own pocket.

This attitude and the infamous practice to which it leads are now fast dying out, but do still occur. Many picture sources will temper their wind to the shorn lamb by reducing their fees when they know that an author is paying for the pictures out of his own pocket; but they do so reluctantly, knowing that it is often the illustrations which make all the difference to the sales of the book. Why, they argue, should they reduce their fees to benefit the publisher? And why should they suffer because an author has been foolish enough to negotiate a contract which leaves him footing the picture bill?

This practice is deplorable, and should be opposed whenever possible. If you as a researcher are involved in such a situation, and find yourself forced to request such reductions, you must expect to encounter reluctance if not downright refusals. Working directly for an author is, in any case, a very fraught business for a freelance researcher: unless he is very well off—which is rare—financial limitations are likely to make your task even more difficult.

Keeping track of costs

It should go without saying that you must keep a meticulous record of the cost of the pictures you obtain, noting the probable ultimate reproduction fee for each picture as you add it to your stock. If not, you may be in for some shocks when the final reckoning comes.

Standard practice is for publishers to pay picture sources when they publish the book, and this is accepted by most sources. You may, however, have to pay some reproduction fees at the time of obtaining the material: this is the case at the National Portrait Gallery and other public collections, where fees must be paid before the material is supplied. As a rule print fees, too, must be paid at the time of ordering. In the case of long-term assignments, some picture sources will ask you to pay an interim service fee (see 2.10) though this will be a fairly small sum simply to cover such costs as have already been incurred.

It is standard practice, too, for sources to bill at the rates current *at the time of billing*. In these days of continually rising costs, and particularly if the project is a lengthy one, there may well have been an increase in rates between the time you obtained the pictures and the time the book is published. You can often offset this by obtaining an agreement from the source for the rates in force *at the time of obtaining the picture*: if the source is reasonably certain that the material will be used, they will generally agree to this. But you must obtain such permission in writing, and keep the document as evidence, for the chances are that the picture source will otherwise forget and follow its standard practice. So, when the time comes for you to inform the source of publication, you ask them to bill you 'at the rate of £x, as agreed in our letter of such and such a date'.

A balancing act

As you see, there are a great number of factors involved in the cost side of obtaining pictures, and experience will teach you to perform a balancing act which will enable you to pick here and there to obtain the best possible pictures at the lowest possible prices. When budgets are really tight, an hour or two comparing various rates cards can help a lot: you will find that a source which is expensive for one type of material is cheap for another, that one source charges more for world rights while another charges a set fee irrespective of market. By juggling these data you can ensure that your money is laid out to the greatest advantage.

Remember that, as a researcher out and about in the field, you are probably more in touch with current rates than is the editor who is employing you: if you think he has made too low an estimate, you should say so, but be prepared to back your assertions with solid evidence, like producing BAPLA's standard recommendations and the rates cards of individual sources. It is then up to him to decide whether to cut down the number of pictures, make do with poorer pictures than he would wish, or increase your budget. If he does none of these things, refuse the job.

3.05 Freelance Researchers' Fees

To establish a fair and at the same time flexible basis for calculating fees for freelance research is not an easy matter. What follows must of necessity be guidelines only.

Basis of payment

There are four possible methods:

● by the hour
● by the day
● by the picture
● by the total assignment, including or excluding reproduction and other fees.

Of these I unhesitatingly recommend the first.

The second can make sense if you go to work full-time on a project, probably operating from your employer's premises as if you were a temporary member of his staff. Since you will be assured of steady and regular work, you may be prepared to charge less for an eight-hour day than for eight individual hours, so both you and your employer may consider this a reasonable arrangement.

The third should be avoided at all costs. There is almost no way in which it can work out fairly to both parties for, while one picture may be found as a result of a five-minute 'phone call, another may require a day or more of hunting. If you are conscientious, you will end up out of pocket: if not, you will cheat your employer by settling for easy-to-find pictures rather than hunting longer for better ones.

The fourth can be appropriate under exceptional circumstances; for instance, when the client has no picture staff of his own and wants to hand over the entire illustration side of a project, so that you become effectively his picture editor as well as researcher. In such a situation it is of course vital that you should ensure that the fee covers all possible costs: in practice it is viable only on a top-quality assignment where cost is a secondary consideration.

Hourly rates

These will of course vary according to the calibre of the researcher. An experienced researcher, who will save her client time and money by her expertise—finding pictures faster and for lower reproduction fees—will expect her expertise to be appropriately rewarded. An acceptable fee in Spring 1979 was £3.50 an hour: down to £3.00 for a relatively inexperienced researcher, up to £4.00 to £4.50 for the more experienced.

A few seconds with your calculator will reveal that £3.50 an hour, for a 40-hour week 48 weeks of the year, works out at £6,720 per annum, which sounds pretty good even with cab rates what they are. But of course no freelance is ever 100 per cent employed, there are gaps between appointments as well as between assignments, and a closer look at those figures shows that a freelance researcher is going to have to work pretty hard to make a decent living and enjoy the rewards of being her own boss.

The cost of a research assignment

Your employer may accept your hourly rate, but he will still want to know what this is likely to set him back for the total job. Once again, there are so many variables that I can offer only guidelines.

Picture rate

A useful starting-point is to reckon on a research time of one hour per picture. In other words, if your editor wants you to find 100 pictures, he must reckon on a research fee of £350, plus or minus. (Spring 1979 figure, not including reproduction fees, print fees or expenses.) Plus or minus what?

Various factors will affect the figure:

Administration

Does he want you to cope with the administration (negotiating fees, invoicing, captioning, returning pictures after publication, credits, voucher copies etc.)? At a rough estimate, administration adds some 25 per cent to the cost of the research assignment, so adjust your fee accordingly: £350 research only, £440 or so including admin work.

Type of picture

To locate and commission a photograph of a family portrait on the wall of a stately home in the Outer Hebrides is not quite so easy as ordering a stock photo of the Taj Mahal by moonlight from a central London colour library. Consider what proportion of easy and difficult pictures your list includes, and adjust your estimate accordingly.

Expenses

Don't forget to make it clear that expenses are something else. There will be bills to cover postage, travel, 'phone calls, print fees, stat fees and the like. If he asks you to give him an inclusive figure, look back at a previous job, see what percentage the expenses represented compared with your research time cost, and make a similar estimate for this job.

If you have a good working relationship with your employer, and particularly if he himself is experienced, he will appreciate that to fix an unvarying sum ahead of time is unrealistic. If he insists on doing so, then he must expect you to pitch the figure somewhat higher than your estimate, to take into account any contingencies (maybe adding, say, another 10–20 per cent). Better for him to accept that the eventual fee will be *in the region* of your estimate, and be prepared to pay slightly more—or even slightly less, you never know!—for the completed assignment. To sum up, your estimate of the research cost will be:

- Basic one hour at your hourly rate per picture
- plus 25 per cent per picture if admin work is required
- plus an additional factor if pictures are unlikely to be easily accessible
- plus percentage to cover expenses
- plus 10–20 per cent contingency margin if you are required to make a firm estimate.

3.06 Obtaining Pictures

Some sources insist on personal visits, others deal only by letter, others expect telephone requests. This is indicated in such guides as *The Picture Researcher's Handbook*. Should you have a choice, each method should be used according to circumstances.

By letter

Use this method:

- when you have a long list of pictures (having established first by 'phone that the list will be acceptable)

● when you have a complex request involving detailed references, foreign names, etc.
● when you have photostats of, or similar to, the pictures you need
● when you are not in a hurry.

Letters should be on the publisher's or on your own printed stationery, and typewritten unless this is absolutely impossible. Handwritten letters, and those on private stationery, will simply not be treated as seriously as the others, and may be totally ignored by a busy source. Letters should contain all essential information and nothing more. That sounds obvious, but you'd be surprised how often essential data is omitted, or padded with extraneous information which obscures the real need.

The source will need to know:

● the name of your company (including address and 'phone number if you're writing on your own letter head and there's a possibility that your employer's address may be unfamiliar to the source)
● the name of the editor (if relevant: this is certainly true of freelance researchers, not necessarily with staff researchers)
● the title of the book or publication, or working title if as yet undecided
● author's name, if relevant
● proposed publication date, date of issue, transmission date: if a periodical, date and/or number of issue
● number of copies to be printed, if known
● rights required, if known
● type of market, if relevant: e.g., if specialist, aimed at sixth formers, designed for international market, etc.
● your name (clearly) and position in the company if staff; if freelance, this should be pointed out.

The picture list

If your list is a long one—say, more than half a dozen items—it is best to present it on a separate sheet. You should not, if possible, send a complete list of all the material you need unless you genuinely think there is a chance that the source can help with a large proportion of it. If the list is long, and it would really be a formidable task to copy it out, indicate on the list the ones you do hope they'll have, or cross out those you expect to obtain elsewhere. The source won't want to wade through a long list hunting for items within their scope, and even if they do make the effort, they may well miss an item, or try to send you something you can get better elsewhere or indeed have already obtained.

● Annotate the list where appropriate. While you can assume that a source will know who Disraeli was or Graham Greene is, they will need to know more about an eighteenth-century architect, or, if you want the Duke of Bedford, *which* Duke of Bedford.
● Which pictures do you want in colour, which in black and white?
● Do you want a photograph, an engraving, a cartoon?
● If asking for, say, the House of Commons, do you want its interior or exterior, in the past or present, animated or architectural?
● If you know of a specific place of origin—e.g., a view of Jamaica which appeared in the *Illustrated London News* in 1932—give the reference, as this may help the source to track down the picture or a near equivalent.
● Always supply photostats if you can, for a visual reference is worth any number of words.

By 'phone

Use this method:

● when you want general information about a picture source you have never used before. Most sources are used to answering queries like 'please tell me how you work' and a 'phone call is the way to find out which method of receiving requests they prefer. You can then decide whether to go on and say 'Well, in that case, could you please send me . . .' or alternatively to send a letter or pay a personal visit
● when you have a short, specific request, e.g., a picture of Columbus on the deck of the Santa Maria, or a portrait of Richard Nixon
● for highly characterised requests of the 'know-what-I-mean?' type, which you need to explain at some length and go on explaining until you feel confident the person at the other end understands you. For instance, you might be looking for 'a pair of nineteenth-century lovers, they must look really romantic, you know, head in the clouds, no sex or anything too physical, see what I mean?'

By and large you should 'phone only when you know that 'phoned requests are acceptable. Obviously, this is more likely to be the case when you have got to know a source and they have got to know you—you just 'phone up and say you're Linda from the *Observer* and can they pop a picture of Lenin in a cab? There need be no more to it than that. But before you can reach this stage you must have established your credentials, for what you are asking them to do is send off their material without any written confirmation of your order.

By personal visit

Use this method:

- when you want to get to know a picture source
- when you need a lot of material, and when you want to avoid a large search fee: indeed, they may prefer you to do your own research in such a case
- when you have a very general brief, and you want to be free to browse in their files (that is, if they provide open access)
- when you must find a picture that is exactly right—one of the French Revolution, say, to go on a book jacket—and you need to look through masses of material to find the one that's just what you want

Of the three methods, a personal visit is always the best if you've got the time, particularly when you don't yet know the source and they don't yet know you. However, though most sources welcome visitors, a minority don't, so always check first. Nearly all sources prefer visitors to come by appointment, even if it is an appointment for later that same day, as there could always be some reason why your visit might prove awkward—they may be too busy, they may have TV cameras in filming, there may have been a flood last night, who knows? So *never* turn up at a source without first making an appointment or checking that you don't need one.

The staff will accept it as part of their job to explain their way of working and to show you where the files and catalogues are, but try not to make any more demands on their time than you have to: however good-natured they are, they are sure to be busy people with many other things to do.

Leave everything as tidy as you find it. If you move a book or a picture, replace it precisely where you found it, even though there seems to be no reason why it should be there rather than anywhere else—the staff may have reasons which you know nothing about! If in doubt, never replace a picture in what could be the wrong place: a wror¬ly filed picture is almost as bad as a lost picture.

Mo picture archives forbid smoking, for obvious reasons. Even if you don't actually see NO SMOKING signs, ask before lighting up.

Make captioning notes as you go along, asking further questions of the staff if you need more information than the picture carries. This can save time in the long run, as by doing it on the spot there is no doubt which picture you are referring to.

Do not take more pictures than you need. That sounds obvious, yet this is a difficult matter: how many is too many? Naturally the source will be delighted if you use a lot of their material: equally naturally, they will be angry if you take a lot but use only a tiny fraction. If the ratio of unused to used is too high, you may be penalised with a service fee. Nor will your employers think much of your powers of selection if you bring back too many.

Note the name of the person who helps you, as, should further queries crop up, it will be better to speak to someone who may remember you and your order.

If they have a photostat machine on the spot, it may be worth taking photostats of dubious items rather than borrowing the originals (see 3.08). This applies also to material in books.

Service fees

Some researchers feel that, because they have carried out their own research, there should be no service fee on the job. They forget that there is a lot more to service than taking pictures out of files—indeed, that is probably the least arduous part of the process. The paperwork, the checking out and checking in again and the re-filing are infinitely more laborious: it is much more irksome putting pictures back in files than taking them out. So if you do your own research you can expect the search/service fee to be lower, but it won't vanish altogether.

From overseas sources

As the world grows more internationally minded, there is no essential difference between ordering material from foreign sources and doing so from your own country: most picture sources are used to handling requests from overseas. At the same time there is an extra dimension of unfamiliarity, chiefly because of differences of language, partly also because working methods do vary from one country to another. It is therefore best, until you know the source well, to send your request in writing. If you can write it, or get a friend to write it in the language of the source, so much the better are your chances of getting what you want.

Remember that names well known to you may be unfamiliar to a foreign source. Your employer may be a household name in Britain, others may never have heard of him. By and large, overseas sources tend to be more formal and go more by the rule book than do British sources: so write in a formal manner, quote every conceivable reference number and date, and be sure to identify yourself, your status and your employer and give all relevant information.

When obtaining material from overseas it is much more likely that you will have to purchase copyprints than be able to borrow material on approval. You will probably be billed for these immediately or even before the material is sent, and must expect to pay for them immediately (it will often be an outside photographer who sends you the bill). You will subsequently inform them what use you have made of the material, in the usual way. Most foreign companies will be ready to handle small sterling cheques, so small sums can be paid in this way: larger payments should be made through a bank.

Returning material to overseas sources

If you have borrowed material—notably colour transparencies —from overseas sources, you will probably want to safeguard yourself against loss when returning it. Small packets with just one or two items can be sent by registered letter post without too much difficulty, but larger shipments can involve you in customs declarations, export licences, proof of their original import, and all manner of red tape: not only does it involve you in much complicated filling of forms, but it also requires you to find out in the first place what forms you have to fill in.

With some hesitation, I'll describe an easier way, though one not without risk. This is simply to pack the material securely in a jiffy-bag, leaving one end openable for customs purposes but securing it firmly with the bend-over kind of paperclips. On the green customs sticker (obtainable from any post office) you write, quite legitimately, PRESS MATERIAL, NO COMMERCIAL VALUE as description of contents and NIL where it asks you to specify value: then simply post in the normal way. Should the material fail to arrive, you will have no recourse and no claim on the Post Office, and will have to bear the full cost of the loss: but the chances of this are small and you may feel the risk is worth taking. It may sound madly foolhardy, but in fact this is based on the experience of two major London picture sources who continually use this method and have had no trouble as a result. However, we take no responsibility for the consequences if you follow this advice.

3.07 Commissioning Photography and Ordering Copyprints

A picture in a library is of no use to a researcher unless she can either borrow it or obtain a copy of it. In this respect, picture sources fall into two classes: those which deal only in photographs, and those which deal in a variety of visual material which may or may not include photographs. Photographic libraries are further subdivided as regards black-and-white and colour collections.

Black-and-white photographic libraries

Here there is no problem with regard to obtaining copies. The material, by its nature, is on negative, enabling prints to be run off as required. The only question is whether the source expects the client to purchase copyprints or borrow them. Some offer the choice. The cost of a copyprint is rarely more than £1.50 (1978), often less, so this is not a major problem for the client. Many sources, such as commercial firms and tourist organisations, while supplying photographs on what is technically a loan basis, do not in practice mind particularly if the prints are not returned and make little effort to retrieve them since it is cheaper to write off the print cost than to employ someone to try to get them back.

Colour photographic libraries

All-colour libraries, or colour departments of other libraries, whose material consists of transparencies, always lend them and virtually never sell duplicates. The reason is that duplicate transparencies, besides being expensive to make, are nearly always inferior to the original.

Given the rapid development of photographic technology, it may not be long before a method is devised of producing duplicate transparencies at low cost and of high quality. I hope someone somewhere is working on this right now.

Non-photographic libraries

A library with non-photographic material may lend out all its material, or some of it, or none of it. 'Some' is the most usual. As the rarity and therefore the value of original material such as engravings increases, there is a growing reluctance to permit original material to leave the library, and a corresponding trend towards having it copied and lending copyprints instead.

This is not such a retrograde step as it may sound. A good copyprint loses little or none of the quality of the original and in some cases actually enhances it, from the reproduction point of view, by boosting contrast and increasing size. It also means that the client is free from the responsibility of working with a valuable and perhaps irreplaceable original. Practice varies with regard to the question of who is to pay for the copying of original material which has not previously been copied. Here are some examples from libraries in London reflecting varying points of view:

The National Portrait Gallery

If a client requests a copyprint of a picture which has not previously been copied, the Gallery will bear the cost of copying itself, charging the client only a print fee. This is because, as a definitive national archive, the Gallery is anxious to build up a complete coverage of portraits on negative.

The Saint Bride Printing Library

If the item has already been copied, the library will charge only a print fee; but if it hasn't the client is expected to pay the copying cost as well. This is because the Library, with its enormous bulk of material in a highly specialised field for which demand is limited, could not possibly afford the cost of putting every item on neg.

Mary Evans Picture Library

This library distinguishes between two classes of picture: those which it is glad to have copied, for possible future use, and those which it is not particularly interested in having copied, because it is improbable that anyone will ever want them again. In the first of these instances they will themselves carry the cost of copying, perhaps adding a small service fee to their normal charge; in the second, they expect the client to pay all or some of the cost of copying, making it tantamount to outright purchase.

Copyprints: buying or borrowing?

Practice varies widely in this respect. For example: The *National Portrait Gallery* does not lend copyprints, but sells them in every instance. This is true of museums in general. The *Radio Times Hulton Library* only lends its copyprints, does not sell them, and insists on their return. *Popperfoto* will lend prints in the first instance but, if they are not returned by a stipulated date, will regard them as having been purchased, and send in an invoice for a print fee. *Mary Evans Picture Library* allows clients either to borrow or buy copyprints, whichever suits them best.

Copying facilities

Every picture source has to have copying facilities of some kind, except in the case of all-colour photo-libraries. The larger sources can of course afford to maintain their own photographic departments, capable of producing copies as required in a matter of minutes. For smaller sources, such facilities are not economically viable, and they have to make do with less satisfactory arrangements as best they can. This generally takes the form of standing arrangements with outside photographers or studios.

Museums and other official collections have in the past tended to employ external facilities but are increasingly setting up or expanding their own photographic departments. In the long run this will undoubtedly be a beneficial development as it will mean that the copying facilities can be integrated with the collection itself to create a streamlined process within the walls of the museum. The ideal will be for every item to be photographed so that all a researcher has to do is quote the reference number and the requisite print is supplied. In the meantime, however, during the transitional period the consequences are long delays and a sorry fall-off in efficiency. At present, if you order a copyprint from most of the big London official collections, you will have to resign yourself to a very considerable wait *whether or not they already have the item on neg*. Sadly it is likely to be some time before a service is generally available to match that provided by the commercial sources. However, the goodwill and helpfulness of the staff will generally make the process as convenient as possible.

It used to be generally possible, and still is so at the *Victoria & Albert Museum* and some other establishments, that you can send in your own photographer (or take a camera in yourself) to copy an item in the collection. In such a case all you pay the museum is an access or facility fee, and subsequently such reproduction and copyright fees as are applicable, all of which are relatively low. The copying fee is paid to the photographer, who retains the negative, though the copyright remains with the museum. The right to reproduce (subject to copyright) is yours as the commissioner of the photograph (see 2.12) though there may be some restrictions such as regarding the use of fine art items in advertising.

Because photographers who work in museums often reckon to do a batch of commissions on each visit, they can keep their costs down, so it is prudent to use a photographer who works regularly in this way rather than commissioning your own photographer to make a one-off visit. At the Guildhall, for example, they have a standing arrangement with John Freeman for black-and-white (he comes in every Tuesday), and with Cooper-Bridgeman for colour. As a typical example of costs, the GLC recommend a photographer who (1977) charged a £4 minimum (plus print fee).

Commissioning a photographer

Most clients who frequently commission photographers will have either staff photographers or professionals whom they employ regularly, sometimes on a retainer basis. It is usually the editor's rather than the researcher's job to commission such material.

Should you be called on, and if there are no in-house facilities, your first problem is to find the most suitable photographer for the type of job. While most photographers probably reckon to be able to photograph almost anything, there is no doubt that some are better at one type of subject than others: the fashion photographer may have no feeling for landscape, the architectural photographer may fail to capture the mood of a social occasion. In such cases, unless you know of a particular individual's work, it is best to approach an agency and ask them to recommend the most suitable individual. Alternatively, look in a directory such as *The Picture Researcher's Handbook* for a photographer who specialises in that kind of work: most photographers accept individual commissions.

When the job is a relatively straightforward one—say, a simple photo of the marketplace at Hexham, Northumberland—you will not want a big-name (or big-price) photographer. You can save a lot on costs by using a man on the spot, and here the IIP (see 1.07) and other professional photographers' associations can be of great help. The IIP register lists photographers throughout the country and indicates their specialities. Besides saving on expenses, a local man will be well placed to take advantage of weather conditions and will have local knowledge of viewpoints, etc.: indeed, he may have just the picture you want already in stock.

An additional reason for choosing a photographer who is a member of a recognised professional body is that, in the event of any dispute, there is a higher authority to which you can appeal. Moreover, such bodies have scales of recommended fees which will give you a guideline as to costs.

When commissioning such a photographer, it is important to brief him fully. Besides such obvious information as the subject and character of the publication in which the photograph is to appear, he may be influenced by the method of printing you will be using (see 4.05, 4.06, 4.07), which may call for greater or less contrast, and by the shape and size of the illustration, if you know this in advance. It will be helpful, too, if—in the case of Hexham marketplace—you can make it clear whether the emphasis is on the architecture, the general ambiance of a country town, or on the kind of people who are to be seen there.

Rights

Be very sure, when commissioning a photographer, that it is clear between you what rights you require. Larger organisations have their own purchase orders on which this is clearly set out. See 2.12 for who owns what rights, unless otherwise specified.

Never forget that the purchase of a copyprint or a transparency does not in itself give you the right to reproduce it, unless you yourself commissioned it. Otherwise, copyright remains with the owner, even when you have bought a copy, and you are legally obliged to obtain permission every time you make use of that picture.

When you commission a photographer, he will retain the negative unless you specifically indicate otherwise in your order. This does not, however, give him any right to use that picture for reproduction purposes.

3.08 Photostats and Polaroids

Photostats

Photostats (sometimes referred to, dangerously, as photocopies, which is apt to confuse them with copyprints, or as xeroxes, after the best-known though by no means the only manufacturer of the appropriate hardware) can be a very useful aid to the picture researcher. Though they are rarely suitable for reproduction, they enable you to take away, at low cost, a visual record of material you have seen in a picture source, without having to borrow the original or order a copyprint, and without having to rely on your written description.

The biggest limitation is that only the most sophisticated machines will copy colour, and none will copy transparencies adequately. What you may be able to do with colour material, however, is to copy a print, or a black-and-white version, of the same picture.

Many sources have their own photostat facilities. Since the equipment is primarily designed for copying documents, the quality is variable, to put it kindly: but you will generally get sufficient resemblance to the original to serve as an adequate reminder. Charges are usually about 8 to 10p per copy, depending on whether the charge includes service or not. Photostats so purchased are your own property, and are not usually returnable.

Some ways in which you can make use of photostats:

● When you wish to have a visual reminder of a picture you have seen, but do not wish to borrow at this stage in the assignment—for example, when you know that the project is a long-term one and you wish to incur neither holding fees on the one hand nor copyprint fees on the other.

● Similarly, when you know you will eventually have to order copyprints or commission photography but are not yet sufficiently sure of what material you will need, so are making a provisional gathering of material to see how it shapes up.

● When you have spotted a possibly useful picture in a book or periodical which you are not permitted to borrow, and which you would like your editor to see before ordering a copy.

● When you are unable to make a personal visit to a picture source—for instance, if it is overseas—but wish to see a wide selection of material on a subject. Thus, the Mary Evans Picture Library invites its overseas clients to order a selection of material on a given subject of general character: they then make two photostats of each illustration, sending one set to the client and keeping the other, numbering both identically. If the client then wishes to order copyprints, he simply quotes the number, thus saving time and money.

● When all you need is general reference material—for example, for artist's references for costume or building styles—stats are often of good enough quality. They can be kept as long as they are needed, drawn on or otherwise marked if necessary, without risk either of holding fees or of damage costs. In such a case, costs will be limited to the price of the stats plus a reference/service fee.

● When you wish to order the original or a copyprint of the item, a stat sent to the source will ensure that you are sent precisely the picture you want. You can even send them a stat of your stat.

● When the immediate purpose of the stat has been achieved, it can be filed for possible future use. A collection of stats can thus be

Camera versus artist. A London night-refuge as seen by Gustave Doré (London, 1871) and, *overleaf*, by an anonymous camera (*Living London*, 1900)

built up which provides you with a useful additional working reference source. Indeed, there is no reason why you shouldn't take stats of any particularly interesting item you come across in a source, perhaps while hunting for something completely different, if you think it likely that it may come in useful on some future assignment.

Polaroid copies

Although not in widespread use, a growing number of picture sources have equipped themselves with Polaroid instant copying facilities which, despite their limitations, provide a valuable back-up to conventional photographic facilities, particularly in respect of time.

The Polaroid MP4 system is a small and compact unit easily housed in all but the most restricted premises, and requires no special conditions such as a dark room. It enables prints to be made in a matter of two or three minutes, for instance from the pages of a book or periodical which you are not permitted to take away.

The big drawback is that the prints are only 12 x 9 cm (5 x 4") in size, which is very small if the original is large. On the other hand the quality is remarkably good: photographs can be copied with no discernible loss of quality, and so can line engravings of the Bewick type. In fact, the Polaroid will copy pictures of virtually any size, but there is naturally a psychological barrier to working to such small reductions when the original is, say 40 cm across. But for pictures where the original is small in any case—such as the Bewick woodcuts already mentioned—the picture does not suffer in any way, and you need have no hesitation in accepting them for reproduction purposes.

3.09 Receiving, Storing and Returning

Receiving pictures

Receiving pictures which you have requested by 'phone or letter, or which are being sent in consequence of visiting a source, would on the face of it seem to be the easiest part of the research assignment. Someone else has done the work, and you simply have to accept the result of their work. Alas, nothing is quite that simple. There are many potential snags even at this stage and, while most of the points

which follow are common sense, it's easy to slip up through care-
lessness unless you start and continue methodically.

As your material accumulates, whether as a response to written or
phoned requests or as a result of your personal researches, check it
off item by item. Look through all material as it arrives and check for
damage incurred during mailing, or possibly already existing when
it left the source. Inform them at once if there is any damage: if you
do not, you may later be held responsible. Check that it really is the
material you asked for. Check it against their delivery note and make
sure it corresponds, that the job number is right and the subjects as
indicated. Do *not* throw their delivery note away!

If you are dealing with a source for the first time, read their conditions and make sure they are acceptable. Some sources expect you
to acknowledge receipt of their material. Do this promptly, to avoid
being bothered with follow-up inquiries. If material has been sent to
you on approval, give it a preliminary look-through at the earliest
possible moment, and return whatever is definitely of no use to you.
Most sources would prefer to have their material returned as
promptly as possible, even if it means getting it back in dribs and
drabs rather than all together.

When you return material, whether all or some, enclose a note telling the source what you are doing—e.g., that you are returning 15
pictures which are definitely not wanted but retaining 5 others for
further consideration. You'd be surprised how many researchers
and editors simply pop pictures into an envelope and mail them to
the source giving no indication as to whether they are being used or
whatever. This only means that you will be chased by the source for
information, so you may as well save everybody's time by supplying
it in the first place.

If you are expecting material from a source and it does not arrive
within a reasonable time, 'phone them to make sure it was dispatched. If there has been some kind of accident, they will want to
know at the earliest possible moment: it may be held against you that
you did not check when the material failed to arrive as expected.

Note whether the material has to be returned by a specified date. If
there is a holding period, enter this in your day-book or timetable, so
that you can request an extension in good time, should you need it.

Make sure that each item is clearly marked as to the source from
which it comes. If there is no caption material on it—e.g., if it is a
copyprint you ordered—caption it right away while your memory is
fresh. It will be your responsibility to make sure there is adequate information for the editor to compose captions from. If you need more
information, now is the time to collect it, noting: subject; location;
artist, photographer, book source, etc., and date. Never write on a

picture which will have to be returned, or mark it in any way. If you have to write on a print, do so lightly in pencil. Transparencies should be labelled on frame or sleeve. Be careful, when so labelling, not to write on anything which is resting on the print or transparency, as this can make an impression which ruins the item.

Storing pictures

Keep a separate file for each assignment you are currently working on, to avoid confusion, and a separate file for correspondence, notes, delivery notes and other material related to that assignment. You should have some kind of timetable or schedule so that you can keep track of the situation at any given moment—what you've got, what is ordered but is still to arrive, what you have yet to find.

Be methodical about how you store material, and ensure it is safeguarded against damage, loss, theft, etc. (See 3.10.) If your employer is responsible for storage and you consider his facilities are inadequate, or that the material is not sufficiently protected, you should point this out, reminding him that lost or damaged pictures can lead to very high bills.

Remember, at this stage, that it may not be you who has to ultimately return the material. So make sure that all the necessary information about terms, conditions, holding periods, etc., is filed with the material itself and is passed on to whoever is responsible.

Selection date

Every publisher has his own procedure with regard to picture selection, but typical practice is to fix a selection date about two weeks before the final design or deadline date, in the case of a book. This gives time for the collection of further material, which may arise because the material you have collected is for one reason or another unsatisfactory, or because fresh requirements become apparent when the illustrations are reviewed.

On-loaning

Most picture sources have a strict rule against passing material on to another client, even though it may be someone else in the same company but working on a different project. The reason is obvious enough: sources need to keep tabs on their material, and on-loaning items confuses their paperwork. If, for instance, someone else from your company sees a picture on your desk and wants to use it on her assignment, you must get in touch with the source and obtain their permission. Usually they'll be only too happy, but they *do* need to be told. (And don't forget to make a note of the transaction in your file.)

Much the same applies to sending material abroad. If you plan to do this, perhaps because another edition is being produced overseas, or that happens to be where your head office or your printers are located, you must clear with the source that this is acceptable to them. Some sources are happy to send their material anywhere, others are more cautious. In most countries, for instance, it is virtually unheard-of for original non-photographic material to be loaned, since the prevailing practice outside Britain and America is to purchase copyprints, clients and printers alike tending to treat all material as if it was theirs to do what they like with. As you might expect, the Dutch tend to treat pictures with respect: not so the citizens of more southerly nations.

Delays in publication

If a book is not published on the date originally planned, it is polite to keep your sources informed, so that they won't come bothering you to know what's happening. This is particularly the case if pictures have been borrowed for a specified period. You may then have to request an extension of the holding period.

Returning pictures

Before returning pictures, check for damage. Most damage to pictures occurs at the printer's, and if any has been incurred you need to know whether it is their fault or yours. So draw it to their attention right away in case there is any come-back from the source. If marks such as printing sizes have been put and left on the pictures, clean them off if you can, and remove masking sheets and other labels. In short, try to return the material in as good condition as when you received it.

Most sources charge for damage as well as for loss. If a print is spoiled because sizing lines have left impressions on it which a camera could pick up, you must expect to pay for it to be replaced—and that means not just the cost of getting the print made, but also of captioning it and, in the case of sources who dry-mount their material, that too. You will also be charged if you have removed caption material from a print or transparency. If a mount or transparency frame is covered with notes, the source will have to remove them before they can make the item available to another client, either by cleaning or re-mounting. Either way, it's time and trouble they shouldn't have to spend, and you may be billed for it.

You'd think it would go without saying that all pictures should be adequately packed before being returned, but a surprising proportion of pictures are insufficiently protected against all the horrid things that can happen to items entrusted to Her Majesty's Mails, let alone those of foreign parts. It is not enough to stick a PHOTO-GRAPHS—DO NOT BEND label on the envelope: some bright spark is bound to prove that they do.

The rule is to pack the material so that it *can't* be bent. Corrugated cardboard is the best reinforcement, being sufficiently strong to protect the pictures and light enough not to add too much to the postal cost. Today there are many different kinds of protective envelope available—Jiffybags, Petapaks and the like—and there is no excuse for not giving a picture the protection it deserves. The cost of a damaged picture, remember, is far greater than the postal charges.

Some sources like their material to be returned by recorded delivery or registered post, and certainly this is an additional safeguard. Others, more fatalistic, think that if a picture is going to be lost, it makes little difference whether or not it is registered: indeed, it may be that registered post, being more attractive to thieves, is *more* vulnerable than normal post. If in doubt, ask the source which they prefer.

Until the material is received back at the source, it is *your* responsibility. Pictures dispatched by the source but not received by you are their responsibility, and if you swear you have never received it there is nothing they can do about it but take your word for it. When it comes to returning, the reverse is true: if they deny getting the pictures back, there is nothing *you* can do about it except check that it was really sent (you or your firm's dispatch department should keep a record of all parcels sent, along with recorded or registered parcel slips) and then hope the Post Office can trace it.

Incidentally, it is worth noting that one London picture library, which has sent or received some 40,000 parcels over the past decade, reckons it has suffered only one or two lost parcels in all those years. Consequently, they are not inclined to think much of 'lost in the post' as an explanation why pictures have not been returned!

Non-returnable material

Material, such as copyprints, which has been purchased for an assignment is something about which different publishers have differing policies. A few will file it methodically, for possible further use on new editions or further assignments on the same subject, thus building up a useful collection of artwork on which they will of course have to pay further reproduction rights if it is subsequently re-used, but no new artwork costs.

When this is the case, it is essential that the material should be clearly captioned with information about the book it was used in, or the assignment it was purchased for, even if it was not ultimately used. Most important, the source of the item should be clearly indicated so that application can be made if someone wants to use the picture again.

Other publishers regard such storage as a waste of floor-space, storage facilities and staff time, and prefer to dispose of the material which, chances are, they won't ever need again. If so, it is considerate to return the no-longer required material to the source, since it might be of use to them. If this is not feasible or would be too expensive, the material may as well be destroyed. Remember, the material is still the original source's copyright and cannot be used without their permission, so you, as the purchaser of the material, should take reasonable care to ensure that it does not fall into the hands of people who may be unaware of the circumstances and suppose that they may make free use of it.

3.10 Loss, Damage and Insurance

From the moment you accept material until the moment you return it you are responsible for its safety. In most cases that responsibility will be taken over by your employer when you have completed your research assignment, if you are working freelance, and if you are working in a firm they will be responsible for overall precautions. But so far as the source is concerned, you are the representative of the company whether you are a staff employee or a freelance, and they will hold you personally responsible unless you can produce a written acceptance of responsibility from someone else. (For this reason, most picture sources like to know the name of your editor so that, in case of difficulty, they have a second person to contact.)

Your employer's premises will almost certainly be adequately covered by insurance, but you should check. If you are a freelance researcher receiving material at your home address you should make sure that you are similarly covered. SPREd will be glad to advise on this matter. It is wiser to spend a few pounds a year on reliable insurance cover than risk having to foot large bills for loss or damage.

While the material is in your possession there are elementary precautions you should take:

● When you have to leave your office, never leave pictures on your desk top where they may be stolen, or on the floor where the cleaners may mistake them for rubbish
● Never perch cups of coffee—or, worse, lemon tea—where they can be knocked over onto pictures
● Never file pictures in any way which could possibly bend or buckle them—this applies particularly to unmounted copyprints
● Never send material to the printer's—or indeed anywhere else—without making sure it is properly protected
● Never leave pictures of any kind, but especially transparencies, in direct sunlight
● Never leave pictures for longer than you can help on a lightbox or under bright light
● Never handle prints and transparencies more than you can help, especially with your fingers, and particularly while eating peanut butter sandwiches . . .

Loss, damage and replacement fees

Clients occasionally object, when faced with a charge for the loss or damage of a picture, that the loss fee is higher than the original cost of the picture. This may indeed sometimes be true, but misses the point. The loss fee is intended not simply to compensate the owner for the loss of the original in terms of its material cost, but must also take into account, firstly, the cost of obtaining the picture: if it is a photo of the Taj Mahal by moonlight, or a rare engraving of the Canale Grande at Venice, such cost could be formidable; if the picture is of a specific event—say, a photograph of an assassination—the cost is incalculable as the picture is irreplaceable. The same may be true of an old print which has been hunted for over a period of years. It must also take into account the cost of making the picture available—the processing, mounting, captioning, cataloguing, filing, and, finally, the loss of profit-potential if the picture is no longer available for future clients. You should bear in mind, too, that a picture in a library is not the same as a picture on its own: it is not a one-off item, but forms part of a comprehensive and ordered collection or sequence, and the loss of one item from that collection may detract from the value of the rest as well.

Most picture sources include mention of loss or damage fees in their rates list. These will cover complete loss, serious damage and partial damage.

Transparencies

BAPLA recommend a minimum of £200 for a lost transparency. Some top agencies will charge more, and for a really exclusive picture the cost could be astronomical. The source should give you an indication when a transparency is of such value; otherwise you have the right to pay no more than the source's standard loss fee as stipulated in their list of conditions.

Transparencies of museum artifacts, colour prints and so forth are not rated as highly as 'live' photographs. A library such as the Mary Evans Picture Library will charge about £8 for the loss of a transparency of a picture whose original is in their possession, about £30 for others (1978).

Prints

As costs and values rise, it is becoming increasingly rare for sources to permit original material to be loaned. Nevertheless such historical collections as the Mansell and the Radio Times Hulton Library, and many smaller specialist collections, still hold a very substantial proportion of original material, and do not always require that it should be copied before being borrowed. This is particularly true where copying would be awkward, or where it would result in a significant loss of quality.

Should such material be lost or damaged, the cost of replacement is not easily assessed. An item may be of small intrinsic value, but the result of intensive searching and could be, in fact, quite a rarity. Consequently, fees in this area vary considerably: the source will usually indicate a minimum fee—'from £10' or so—but charge more in special cases.

In the case of black-and-white copyprints the cost is little more than a replacement fee, plus a charge for the trouble of captioning, mounting and filing the new print. A copyprint loss fee may be as little as £3.

If lost pictures are later found

If pictures which have been lost, and their loss paid for, are subsequently recovered, you must bear in mind that the fact that you have paid a loss fee for them does not mean that you now own them. They are still the source's property and must be returned immediately.

The source will be glad to have the material back, and will generally repay the loss fee in part, or give you a credit for the amount. But they have the right, if they have in the meantime replaced the picture, to deduct the cost of replacement, or to make a deduction in proportion to the period during which the picture was lost, as compensation for being deprived of it. This is more or less tantamount to a holding or blocking fee and the usual rates are: as recommended by BAPLA—10 per cent of loss fee for each month or part of month; as recommended by IIP—25 per cent of loss fee for each quarter year or part of quarter year.

3.11 Rights and Invoicing

By 'rights' is meant the extent of the permission-to-use that a source grants its clients. Unless otherwise specified, permission to use a picture is assumed to be a one-time reproduction right, which BAPLA defines as 'Permission to reproduce one illustration once in one edition of one publication in one language in an agreed territory for a limited time and stated print run'. If you require any elaborations or extensions of this, they must be specified when requesting permission to use. They may include:

- larger than minimum size; e.g. whole page
- use in special positions; e.g. cover, jacket, endpapers
- other editions, such as paperback or translation
- other markets and territories

Rights and rates

The rights you require will correspond, more or less, with the rates on your source's rates card. The way in which the infinite variations are broken down varies from one source to another, so the following structure is only an example of what you are likely to encounter:

BOOKS (first edition only)

A *Originating in UK or any one country except USA*
1   UK or one country only
2   English language excluding USA + Canada
3   English language excluding USA
4   UK and USA only
5   English language including USA
6   Each additional language
7   World, including all translations

B *Originating in USA*
  8 USA only
  9 All English language
 10 World, including all translations

C *Surcharges*
 11 Subsequent editions
 12 Frontispiece, endpapers, back cover
 13 Jackets, covers
 14 Dummies, layouts

Clearly no rates card, however sophisticated, can quote for every combination of rights which may be required: the variations of size, position, edition and distribution are virtually infinite. But from such a structure as shown above it should be possible to calculate any usual requirement.

What constitutes an edition?

An edition is one publication of a work. Every variant constitutes another and separate edition, even though it may be issued at the same time:

- softbound edition of hardbound book
- abridgement
- revision
- translation
- co-edition in another market

In principle, separate or additional fees may be due for each of these new editions. In practice, most sources allow a reasonable degree of flexibility, and it is not customary for additional fees to be paid when, for example, a further printing is made of the same book without change of format. If, however, the fee is based on the length of the print run, an additional fee may be payable if that print run is substantially extended.

A publisher may, if he thinks he may want to market his book in several different formats, choose to negotiate comprehensive rights from the outset, as this can usually be done on more favourable terms than if each edition has to be paid for separately.

World rights

In principle, 'world rights' implies that the picture may be used in any country in the world. This is usually taken to include foreign language editions, whether issued by the same publisher or by some other publisher in agreement with the one you're working with. It is often taken, furthermore, to cover all subsequent editions of those books—paperbacks, abridgements, etc.

However, some picture sources interpret the coverage differently. While the majority are willing to settle for a relatively low initial overall fee which will save having to re-negotiate and re-invoice every time a new right is called for, there are others who impose some reservations on the blanket coverage. So do not assume any situation, and establish that you and your source are speaking the same language before you go ahead and publish.

Exclusive rights

There is normally no legal prohibition to prevent a source allowing two clients to use the same picture at the same time. The only restraint is the ethical one—plus the thought that by so doing they may lose the goodwill of both clients!

Sometimes, however, a publisher will ask for exclusive rights, which means that the source will undertake not to supply that picture to any other client, in the same area and/or same category (e.g. to any other British book publisher). A time limit (say three years) is normally specified, and understandably a higher fee is customarily charged.

Dummies and promotional material

Reproduction fees do not cover additional uses such as advertising or use in catalogues or display material. An additional fee of 50 per cent of the normal fee is frequently charged for such use, though in minor cases the source may waive its right to impose such charges.

A similar rate is customary when the picture is used in a publisher's dummy—that is, when a specimen section of a proposed book is made up so that potential co-publishers and the like can get a good idea what the finished book will look like. This is common practice nowadays for encyclopedias and other high-cost projects, where it is essential for the publisher to find others ready to commit themselves to sharing the cost.

Permission to use

In principle, no publisher should proceed to publication without first obtaining formal permission from each source that their pictures may be used. In practice, many publishers assume that the supplying of the pictures in itself implies such permission: but this is not strictly true, and if sources accept this short-cut it is only to save time and trouble. The more punctilious and prudent publishers will never proceed to publication without formally clearing all permissions.

In some firms it is the editor's rather than the researcher's job to obtain such permission; but it is important that you should establish whose responsibility it is. Failure to clear permission, especially where other than the simplest rights are involved, can have unfortunate consequences.

Since the information as to rights, etc., which you have to supply to the picture source to obtain permission is the same information they require for invoicing, the two processes are generally telescoped. The source may be invited to invoice then and there, if publication is imminent, or is informed of the publication date so that they can in due course invoice on the basis of the information you are providing. Typically, a letter embracing the following points will be sent to the source, generally on a printed form:

- title of book
- publication date
- we request permission to reproduce the following pictures . . .
- subject
- reference number if applicable
- colour/black-and-white
- size reproduced and/or special positions (e.g. frontispiece)
- format (e.g. hardback, softback, etc.)
- approximate selling price
- rights required
- length of print run
- please invoice now/on date above, at . . .

Invoicing

The researcher is in the position of knowing more about the transaction than anyone else does, so you must be familiar with customary invoicing procedure. Some sources, particularly museums and other public collections, insist on payment of reproduction fees before they will grant permission for their pictures to be used, and indeed often before they will supply the pictures at all. Commercial sources, normally, do not expect to be paid until publication, knowing that changes may occur up to the last minute.

As soon as you have certain information as to the use you will be making of the source's material, you should inform them, as they like to know what's going on even though it is still too soon to invoice. At this stage you can inform them when publication is likely to be, and whether you want them to invoice you now or later.

While as a rule publishers, like everyone else, would prefer not to pay any bills until they have to, there is one good reason for sometimes settling bills before publication date. This is that, unless previous agreement has been made, invoicing is at the rate current at the time of invoicing. In these days of continually rising prices, that rate may well go up during the period which elapses between research and publication, so that your employer may find himself being billed for amounts in excess of your original budget. The earlier the source send in their bill, the lower it is likely to be.

Assuming that the source has been properly informed of the date of publication, and has invoiced promptly, payment should be made within one month of publication or invoicing. In practice, the majority of publishers prefer to clear up invoices promptly, as this simplifies their book-keeping.

If you go ahead and reproduce a picture without informing the source, obtaining formal permission and agreeing fees, they will have the right to charge the full amount at their current rates at the time of invoicing, and if they do not learn the situation for a substantial period, it is possible that their rates will have increased not only over what they were when you did your research, but also over what they would have been if they had invoiced at the time of publication. Nor, under such circumstances, are they likely to lend a sympathetic ear to an appeal for a reduction!

3.12 Credits and Voucher Copies

Every illustration you reproduce should have with it some indication as to the source which supplied it. The only exceptions are when pictures are used in advertisements or exhibitions, where such information is not easily accommodated: in cases where no credit is supplied, it is customary to pay a higher fee.

The reason for the higher fee is simple: the picture credit is the finest testimonial a source can have. When the world sees a picture and notes that it comes from such-and-such a source, that is more positive proof of that source's viability than any publicity or promotion, for it constitutes an endorsement by you, the satisfied customer. Moreover, this is no less true of museums and other non-commercial sources: all, in one way or another, are proud of their reputation.

For this reason, sources are always angry when credits are omitted or mistaken. Though to you and your editor and designer and printer they are a nuisance, they are a fact of life you must learn to live with. It is a measure of their importance that some American sources add a 25 per cent surcharge if the credit is omitted.

However, there is more to credits than publicity for the source: they are also of great help to the publisher, and to the researcher in particular. If you see a picture in a book which you would like to use in your current assignment, it saves everyone's time if, thanks to a credit line, you can go direct to the source from which it was obtained, rather than get in touch with the publisher and ask him to check his sources, which can be a time-consuming process especially if it is some time since the book was published. A well annotated book thus becomes a useful research tool in its own right.

Wording of credits

This is usually up to the picture source, who often indicate their preferred wording in their list of conditions. Usually the most common name of the source is used: e.g. *British Library* or *Bibliothèque Nationale*. Sometimes you will have to credit a particular collection within a source, so may have to include such words as *Library of Congress, Brady Collection*. Similarly, when you use a photograph from a photo agency, you may be required to credit both the agency and the individual photographer: e.g., *'Picturescope/John Smith'*. Another complication is when an object in a museum has been photographed by an outside photographer, where again a dual credit may be required: e.g. *'Universitetsbiblioteket Oslo/Jens Olsen'*.

Credit may be required also for the supplier of properties loaned for photography.

Positioning

This is generally a matter of publisher's usage, and varies from one publishing house to another. Alternatives include:

● In small print alongside the picture itself, often vertically up one side. Some photographers insist on this.
● At the end of the caption accompanying the picture, often in italics and/or brackets.
● Elsewhere on the same page or spread, perhaps in the margin or gutter.
● Incorporated with the list of illustrations at the front of the book, usually on the page following the contents page.

● As a separate list of acknowledgements or picture credits, grouped together at the end—or less frequently the beginning—of the book. This is most usual for heavily illustrated books such as those produced by *Reader's Digest* or *Mitchell Beazley*.

Practice also varies as to how the credits are indicated. Some do it by page number, working their way through the book specifying each picture as it comes, with an indication as to whether the top or bottom or right or left hand picture is being referred to. This makes references very easy, but has the disadvantage that the same source may have to be listed many times over, even though abbreviations are customary.

Alternatively the sources may be listed, usually alphabetically, and alongside them the pages on which their pictures are to be found. This is simpler and occupies less space, but is awkward if you're trying to trace a particular picture. Where the bulk of the illustrations come from a particular source, it is usual to say something like 'all illustrations from the *John Johnson Collection* except as otherwise specified', and then list the exceptions.

Because of the importance of crediting, it is most essential that you should be absolutely certain from which source each of your pictures was obtained, and, if you are given the opportunity, check the proofs to make sure no mistake has been made in the attribution.

Credit for researchers

It is becoming more customary for credit to be awarded to the picture researcher, along with the editor, designer and other important contributors, usually on the reverse of the title page. Occasionally, when the researcher is substantially responsible for the book, you may even get your name on the title page. Though this is not yet recognised as a right, it is certainly fitting that good work should be acknowledged, and that when a researcher has played a positive part in the creation of the book she should receive due credit.

Voucher copies

In principle every picture source expects and is entitled to a copy of the publication in which its material appears. This is so that they may check that the picture is being used honourably, that credit has been correctly given, and that the size and other details of use are as agreed. A picture gallery, for instance, might want to be sure that its painting has not been so badly reproduced that it will reflect badly on the gallery itself.

It is generally the editor's job to see that each source receives its voucher copy, but this is not necessarily the case and you should see it as part of your responsibility to check that each of your sources receives its copy, or that your editor undertakes to provide them.

A problem inevitably arises when many sources have contributed to a heavily illustrated and high-priced publication. Under such circumstances most sources, if they have contributed only two or three pictures to a book selling at £10, will accept that it is asking a lot to expect the publisher to provide them with a copy, and a page proof or even a photostat may be acceptable. But these should be regarded as exceptions to the general rule, which is that every contributing source should receive a copy before publication.

Clearly, too, this should be done at the earliest possible moment, so that if the source has any cause for objection, they can voice it before the book is presented to the public, though indeed by this time it may be too late to make changes. But at least it can prevent the disaster which is every editor's ultimate nightmare, total recall of a book once it has been published.

3.13 The Television Assignment

While many of the problems faced by a picture researcher in television are the same as those facing her colleague in the book business, there are obviously certain other factors to be taken into account. Ideally, the job deserves a book on its own. Here, for the moment, is a television picture researcher's assignment programme in outline. Some of the points have been covered in greater detail in earlier chapters: others are specific to the television medium. No researcher would be expected to know these in detail without special training, but this outline does at least indicate how the television researcher's job overlaps with, and differs from, that of researchers in other fields.

● Obtain or prepare picture list, with as much detail as possible.
● Establish what budget has been allocated.
● Check library, cuttings files, etc., to see what has been used before on the subject, noting sources used when indicated.
● Prepare lists of material required and send to sources, giving details of project, author, probable transmission date and any other relevant facts. Indicate whether colour or black-and-white pictures are required. State what rights will be required (e.g., UK only; UK & Commonwealth; World).

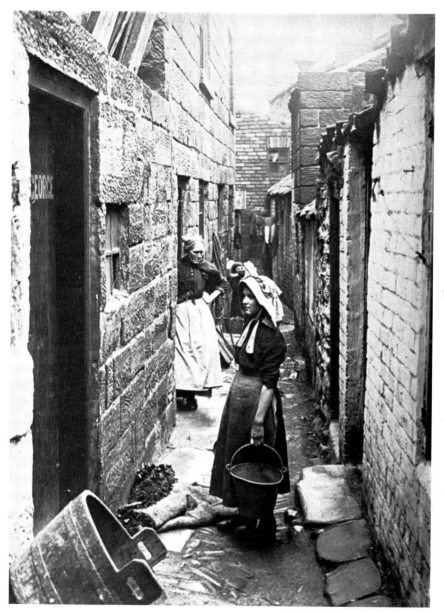

An old photograph, even of poor quality, can have far more visual impact than one taken of the same scene today. This photograph of nineteenth-century back-to-back houses at Staithes, Yorkshire, captures the atmosphere and realism of slum life as no modern photograph could

Often government bodies, public institutions and commercial companies will supply illustrative material at little or no cost. This striking piece of artwork (the original is in colour), showing the separation of an atmospheric probe from an orbiting craft in a mission to Jupiter provisionally planned for launch in January 1982, is from NASA

- Wherever practicable, pay personal visits to sources where you expect a wide selection of material to be available.
- Note that for some types of programme, particular formats will be suitable. For example, on an arts programme where a specific work of art may be discussed in detail, a 25 × 20 cm (10 × 8″) transparency is preferred because it provides better rostruming possibilities. If black-and-white material is required, note that some agencies will provide screen dimension size prints.
- As material comes in, check that it tallies with the source's delivery note, and check off on your own list.
- When material is all or nearly all in, sort it into programmes or sequences. Show it to the director to check that he can, for example, make satisfactory sequences with what you have: check, too, that the cost is within the budget.
- Prepare stills for rostrum cameraman, with accompanying shot list. Mount tracing paper on stills according to screen dimensions. Mark each picture with programme, sequence and still number, and provide shooting instructions for rostrum cameraman—e.g., 'Hold A 5 secs', 'Pan A–B 5 secs', 'Zoom into face of main subject in C'.
- When shooting is completed, stills are returned to the production office, film sent when processed to the cutting room.
- Stills are stored in the production office, in the order in which they were rostrumed, in case any sequence needs to be re-shot.
- When the film is complete, make list of stills used, noting their sources. Inform each source which of their stills are being used, giving details of rights, and request invoice, to be paid after transmission.

PART FOUR
PICTURE SELECTION

4.01 The Varieties of Visual Material

The picture researcher's job has two sides to it—'where' and 'which'. Your primary task is to locate *where*, say, a portrait of Karl Marx is to be found: then comes the task of choosing *which* of the available portraits is most suitable for your need.

On any given subject you are likely to have a choice. Sometimes it will be a choice between a number of roughly similar pictures—a dozen press photos, say, of the launch of the QE2, or a selection of engravings of Rouen Cathedral in the 19th century. But there is also a choice between different ways of looking at a subject. The Boer War, for instance, was recorded both in photos and in engravings made from artists' sketches: both have their advantages, and the nature of your assignment will dictate which you choose—the photographs for authenticity (up to a point!) or the drawings for on-the-spot action, in that epoch uncatchable by the camera. Again, if you are asked for a portrait of a leading statesman like President Carter, you can choose a news photo, a formal portrait done in a studio, or a caricature which may be friendly or hostile depending on your point of view.

It is at this stage that the researcher's job ceases to be simply a tracking-down exercise and becomes an act of creativity. Faced with a choice of visual material, you have to decide which aspect to go for.

Authenticity at all costs

A news photo, if it exists, is what you want, *but* you will have to remember that even if the camera cannot lie, the photographer who holds it can. Remember that the film clips you have seen showing the link-up of the Russian armies round Stalingrad in World War Two are not real but fake; because of the speed of the event itself there was no time to record it at the time, so it was re-enacted, on a scale to draw admiration even from a Cecil B. de Mille, to provide the essential record. Who can say what phony elements may not have crept into the version we now see?

A general impression of the subject, made as vividly as possible

For example, a contemporary artist's impression of the landing of Columbus in the West Indies would fulfil this, *but* you will have to remember that just because it was done at the time, it does not follow that it is accurate. A modern reconstruction, thoroughly researched and conscientiously executed, is more likely to be authentically accurate than one done, however elegantly, by De Brij in 1597.

The 'feel' of the period

A contemporary woodcut illustrating a medieval theme somehow seems more in keeping than a modern reconstruction. If this is what you're after, then you'll prefer De Brij's version of the Columbus landfall, however inaccurate, to the modern version, however accurate.

Suitability for reproduction

Often the finest pictures may have to be rejected because the printing won't do them justice. The picture researcher cannot ignore such mundane considerations.

Choosing a particular slant

For instance, when your author asks for a picture of fox hunting, does he want it depicted as a glorious sport or a cruel pastime? You will be able to find pictures which show it in such a way as to support either viewpoint.

Design considerations

If a picture is to be used small, the designer won't want too much detail which will be lost in reproduction. If it is to be blown up to cover a double-page spread, then it must be able to stand such enlargement. If you don't know in advance, it is prudent when choosing a picture to procure one which will not suffer overmuch either in reduction or enlargement. Even so, it is possible that when the book reaches design stage you will be asked to find an alternative version to meet layout requirements.

To meet these various needs, the picture sources offer you a wide and often bewildering variety of visual material, much of which is some distance removed from 'pictures' as we normally think of them. Besides the various types of illustration—photographs, prints, drawings and paintings—there are, among others: advertisements, antique vase paintings, architect's drawings, artifacts of all kinds, auction catalogues, ballad sheets, bookplates, broadsheets, caricatures, cartoons, cave paintings, children's pop-up books, cigarette cards, cinema stills, coins and medals, comic strips, covers of books and magazines, ephemera of all kinds, exhibition catalogues, fashion plates, graffiti, greetings cards, handbills, holiday snaps, instruction manuals, lantern slides, magazine illustrations, manufacturers' catalogues, maps, menu cards, mosaics, murals, music covers, news photos, official documents, packaging, playbills, postage stamps, posters, pottery and porcelain objects, private photo albums, printers' specimens, record albums, scraps, sculptures and statues, silhouettes, stained glass windows, stereo slides, tapestries, theatre programmes, tickets, timetables, title pages, travellers' souvenirs, trade cards, trade samples, and wall signs.

Some picture sources limit themselves to only one type of material: this is particularly true of modern colour libraries which stock nothing but transparencies. But others, particularly in the historical field, gather together material of various kinds which can save you making too many individual visits. The National Portrait Gallery, for instance, will have caricatures as well as 'serious' portraits, and the paintings it hangs on its walls are backed by files of prints in the archives behind. The *Guildhall* has playing cards, broadsheets, mayoral menus. The Mary Evans Picture Library supplements its 'straight' picture files with such oddities as bookplates, Valentines, trade cards and postcards. And then of course there are sources which specialise only in the unusual, such as music covers or trades union banners.

These matters are discussed more fully in the sections which follow. The important thing is for you to keep yourself aware of the possibilities open to you. When collecting material for a book on highwaymen, say, don't think only of the 'usual' prints, but also of

- film stills, showing how the subject has been treated by the film industry
- modern photographs of Blackheath or Maidenhead Thicket, showing what their favourite haunts look like today and enabling today's reader to link their activities with his own experience
- posters offering rewards for capture of a highwayman
- music covers and ballad sheets representing the highwayman as a popular hero
- relevant artifacts in museums, such as the kind of pistol a seventeenth–century highwayman would have carried.

Using your imagination like this to broaden the field will not only lead to a more original and interestingly illustrated book but also make your research task more exciting, besides giving your employer a higher opinion of your ability and initiative.

4.02 Selecting for Documentary Value

The first criterion in picture selection is normally: does this picture get across the message that the author (or whoever) wants to convey?

Sometimes the message is so straightforward that you can hardly go wrong—for instance, if it is 'The Leaning Tower of Pisa looks like this'. But what if you are asked to say 'Brighton beach looks like this'? Even when you've established that what is wanted is a contemporary photograph, you will still need to be told whether the picture is intended to show what a gorgeous place Brighton is, or how foolish people are to congregate on a crowded beach when they could enjoy more privacy elsewhere, or to show the geological characteristics of the Sussex coast, or . . .

And even that is comparatively simple. What if the picture's message is 'Adolf Hitler looked like this'? Does your author want him young, as a struggling politician, or old, as the leader of his country? Does he want him kindly, accepting a bouquet from a curtseying schoolgirl in peasant costume, or ruthless, haranguing the crowds from the Nürnberg platform? Shrewdly machiavellian as he confers with Eden or Chamberlain, or as the affectionate private man relaxing at Berchtesgarten with Eva? As the German people saw him, the shining leader who would lead them out of the slough of the 'twenties into the glory of the New Order, or as the enemy saw him, a silly little man with a toothbrush moustache biting the carpet? Every one of these is Hitler.

Today we are usually anxious to see the world 'as it really is', and respect Cromwell for instructing his portraitist: 'Mr Lely, I desire you would use all your skill to paint my picture truly like me, and not flatter me at all; but remark all these roughnesses, pimples, warts, and everything as you see me, otherwise I will never pay a farthing for it.' But for all Cromwell's honesty, 'warts and all' reality is only one form of reality. If you fail to notice the blemishes on your lover's face, how 'real' are they? If Cromwell's admirers did not notice his warts, if Hitler's followers saw him as a knight in shining armour, are their views not as valid as that of the all-seeing nothing-hiding camera eye?

So there is a difference between the statements 'The Eiffel Tower looks like this' and 'President Carter looks like this'. Those who regarded the Eiffel Tower as a hideous monstrosity—as many did when it was first erected in 1889—no doubt saw it very differently from its admirers, but the difference was in the eye of the beholder.

Whereas, with President Carter, your choice of pictures can easily depict him as either Folk Hero or Country Yokel.

Contemporary or reconstruction

Representations of historical scenes and events present the same problem in an extreme form. There are obvious attractions in depicting medieval life by using, say, pictures drawn from manuscripts, chronicles, stained glass windows and other artifacts dating more or less from the period.

But make no mistake about it, such pictures show the life of the period not as it 'really' was but as the artists chose to see it, no less than if future generations were to see our own world only as depicted by the artists of today. As information about the objective appearance of the medieval world, such representations are inadequate and even misleading.

If we really want to show what life looked like in medieval times, we shall do far better to re-create it in the form of a modern reconstruction, briefing a competent artist with all the information gathered by archaeologists and historians, with reference material taken from artifacts in museums and all the advantages that modern science can lay on. Books such as those on early civilisations produced by *Time-Life* in their *The Emergence of Man* series provide us with what is probably the most complete and accurate account of what the ancient world 'really' looked like that it is possible to obtain until a time machine is invented.

But not every publisher can afford investment in research and artwork on that sort of scale; and even if they could, they would not necessarily wish it. For even the *Time-Life* type of reconstruction, excellent as it is, is only a partial reconstruction. It shows the surface appearance of the ancient world splendidly—but it shows that appearance as we, inhabitants of the twentieth century, would see it. Seen through the eyes of a contemporary, it may have looked emotionally quite different, despite the accuracy of the surface detail. For this reason there is still a strong preference for the contemporary depiction of the scene, with all its distortions and deficiencies. What it gives us may be factually incorrect, but emotionally it is in harmony with its subject.

In practice, when hunting for historical material, the researcher is apt to be presented with an even more perplexing version of this dilemma. What is frequently available from historical picture sources is neither a contemporary engraving or whatever, nor a modern attempt at re-creation, but a reconstruction made in the nineteenth century. On the face of it, such versions, usually in the form of a wood engraving as used in British, French or German history books of the period, present the worst of every possible world: they are neither contemporary in ambiance, nor have they the accuracy of a modern reconstruction. We may give their creators the benefit of the doubt and suppose that they did their best with the materials then available, but they had not the benefit of the vast amount of archaeological and historical research which has been carried out in the subsequent hundred years. Inevitably a Victorian artist's conception of the landing of Julius Caesar on the British coast was made up largely of imagination, only slightly diluted with dubious fact. And yet it remains true that such illustrations do often present a very acceptable compromise: not only the worst of both worlds but also something of the best—a vague 'historical' feel which does not clash too harshly with its subject, yet without the ludicrous distortions of genuinely contemporary material.

Once again, the decision is going to be a subjective one, and it will be up to you as researcher to gauge your author's intentions and try to match them with your picture selection.

Often, of course, the true picture simply does not exist in any form. Frequently the actual facts were unknown or concealed at the time: for instance, it is not at all easy to find pictures of poor factory conditions during the Industrial Revolution. Should we tell the history of the railways in terms of railway accidents, or chronicle the story of the theatre in terms of box-office flops?

When selecting pictures for their documentary value, you will be looking for truth. But you will have to be clear in your mind *which* truth, from the many alternatives available, is the truth you want. You will need to be sure that your idea of the truth is the same as your author's. And then you will have to look for an artist or a photographer whose vision of the truth matches yours.

4.03 Selecting for Aesthetic Value

Why are some pictures reproduced over and over again, even though there are alternatives available which offer just the same quantity of informative detail? Why are Gustave Doré's scenes of London life used so frequently, despite their obvious exaggerations? Why are Cartier-Bresson's glimpses of human behaviour chosen time and time again despite the fact that the world is full of competent photographers? What is it that makes Bewick's woodcuts of animals stand out above any others?

Critics could no doubt analyse the factors that give these three artists their pre-eminence. But even without such analyses, we feel there are qualities in their work—'something about them'—which give them an extra appeal over and above their value as visual documents.

Not everyone will agree in every case. The Canadian photographer Karsch of Ottawa is regarded by some as the greatest portrait photographer of all time, while others deride his work as cold and sterile. And when it comes to paintings, judgments are even more subjective—remember how Churchill hated Sutherland's portrait of him! To what extent can the picture researcher afford to indulge or impose her personal taste?

The aesthetic value of a picture is made up of three factors:

The intrinsic qualities of the individual picture

The way the subject-matter is arranged, the balance of the contents, the way colour is used, the formality or fluidity of the line. All these are elements which go to make up the total impact of the picture: they may be subject to analysis, they may even lend themselves to teaching by rote, but ultimately they are the instinctual response of the artist to his subject, and must be matched by an instinctual response on the part of the public—for whom you, as the researcher who has to choose the picture, stand as a representative. It is your taste, combined with your experience, which will determine whether you choose this picture or that.

The qualities inherent in that category of picture

There is a special appeal in a medieval manuscript, a 17th-century woodcut, an 18th-century French erotic engraving, which conveys a 'feel' that nothing else can. Those meticulous steel engravings of early Victorian landscapes, so wonderfully adapted to the contemporary cultivation of the romantic temperament, evoke a quite different response from that created by paintings or water colours of the same subjects—you have only to compare a Turner painting with a steel engraving of the same subject to feel the difference, each valid in its own way. Those formal late Victorian photographs, demanding to be printed in sepia, have a 'quality' about them which no modern photograph, no matter how painstakingly set up, ever seems quite to capture.

Certain types of picture come in and out of fashion: they seem, somehow, to reflect a period or a mood. An example is the poster. In the 1890s there was a tremendous boom in poster design: collectors

vied with one another to obtain the newest Chéret, Steinlen or Tou-
louse-Lautrec, magazines were published in their praise, artists like
Will Bradley were, if not household names, respected figures in the
artistic world. Then, with a few exceptions, the poster as an art form
disappeared for half a century, only to be rediscovered within the last
two decades. Today you have only to look on the bookshelves of any
art shop to see what a boom there has been in poster art, something
which would not have been thought fit for serious consideration a
quarter of a century ago. Today it is recognised that the poster—
designed to be 'read' on a distant wall or seen from a passing 'bus—
has its own inherent qualities quite different from those of a picture
designed to be admired on a gallery wall or studied in a book or
magazine.

The context in which the picture will be used

Ultimately this is going to be up to the editor and his designer, but
you can make valuable contributions at the research stage. Start by
discussing the book with the editor or designer, to understand how
they 'see' the book. Some illustrated books are no more than collections of pictures, just slapped down on page after page, the publisher's only concern being that they should contain the visual
information required. But a well produced book will go further than
this; it will generate its own climate, manipulate the way in which
readers respond to it, by the way the pictures are used and arranged.
By juxtaposing pictures, by bleeding some off the edge of the page,
by using tints and screens and decorative borders and ornamental
initials, by enlarging some pictures and reducing others, by playing
off visual against type matter in a dynamic rather than a neutral way,
the designer can use pictures creatively to make the book as a whole a
response-creating object. If you, as a researcher, can sense the mood
the designer is seeking to establish, you can help him by selecting
pictures which will confirm that mood.

Perhaps the best way you can help is by looking for variety. Books
which contain lots of the same type of picture presented in the same
way page after page give the designer no scope; he will need all his
expertise to prevent the book becoming visually monotonous and so
emotionally tedious.

So let's imagine that you have been asked to collect pictures for a
book on Wagner.

Naturally you'll start with pictures of Wagner, his family, his
friends and his associates. You will choose some photographs, some
paintings, some drawings, some caricatures. Some photographs will

be mounted on the original photographer's mounts, with gilded edges and decorative printing: you will retain this for its period flavour, not to mention the interesting point that it was made while he was passing through Prague . . . There will be group scenes, and some in which some kind of interaction is taking place between the figures—looking at each other, eating, at the piano and so on. Some will be formal, others casual. Don't be afraid to include poor quality photographs if they help to create atmosphere—sometimes a casual 'snap' is more revealing than a formal portrait.

Wagner's homes, and the theatres in which his works were performed, can be shown both from old prints and photos and in modern photographs. It is of course interesting to see pictures of München and Bayreuth as they were in the days when he lived there, but modern colour photographs of them as they are today help us to remember that these are living, real places.

Scenes from the operas can take many forms. There will be wood engravings of the earliest performances: perhaps some better quality lithographs, softer in texture and more pleasing to the eye. Later, when Wagner was famous, perhaps some artist painted scenes from performances. There will be rough sketches by the stage and costume designers. There will be black-and-white photographs of later performances, colour photographs of modern productions, film stills from cinema versions. There will be newspaper headlines about the first performance of *Lohengrin* in Paris and other such incidents: there will be programmes and playbills, posters and contemporary reviews from the papers which can be reproduced in their original typefaces. All of these will add texture: but not only will they divert the eye and keep the reader's mind active, they will also help to set Wagner's work in its period and give today's reader a sense of the age in which it was produced.

Apart from the material content, shape can help. Many old photographs were presented in an oval shape which can soften the look of a page by offsetting the formal lines of type. Mixing upright and landscape pictures gives variety. Old photographs and engravings can often be vignetted—made to go blurry round the edges—which again gives a soft look. If you know the designer has this sort of effect in mind, you can select illustrations which lend themselves to such treatment.

Ephemera is another helpful way of adding texture—the invitation card to a first night, tickets to the theatre, the menu at a birthday party, the hotel bill when Wagner stayed at Bonn . . . This type of material is not generally kept in the open files of most picture sources because of its rarity and fragility but, if you show a genuine interest, the staff may be encouraged to dig it out.

To carry out an assignment in this kind of way can turn picture research into a truly creative activity, much more satisfying than working from a typed list with no indication as to how the pictures are to be used. Often—perhaps in the majority of cases—there isn't much you can do. But whenever you get the chance look for the opportunity to make both your work and the finished product more rewarding.

4.04 Selecting for Reproduction Quality

A picture may look magnificent, it may express perfectly the author's intention, but if it cannot be reproduced it is useless. This is where picture research comes back down to earth with a dismaying thump.

The documentary and aesthetic values of a picture both call for the researcher's personal judgment and taste, but the question of suitability for reproduction is a matter of impersonal technical skill. You will not be expected to be expert in this skill, but you *will* be expected to have a general notion of what is entailed.

This means knowing which kinds of picture reproduce better than others, and under what circumstances; from which it follows that you must acquire some knowledge of what is entailed in reproduction processes. The courses in picture research organised by such bodies as the Publishers' Association include a visit to a printer, and cover most of the everyday problems of reproduction. Whether or not you have the opportunity of attending such a course, you should endeavour to acquire such knowledge. In the sections which follow we set out a certain amount of basic information which should be helpful, but you should try to supplement this with a visit to a printer if you can fix it.

Don't get the idea, though, that knowing the processes and the problems will give you a nice neat set of rules to work to. There will still be room for flexibility. There will be times when you will need to use a picture even when you know it will not reproduce well. Thus the only pictures of the Russian royals in captivity in 1918, for instance, are of poor quality—but they are the best available. You will have to decide whether it is better to use such unique material, despite its lack of quality, or get an artist to make an impression. Sometimes, indeed, you can even make a virtue out of poor-quality reproduction. A blurred action photograph, out-of-focus and badly lit, of some such event as the Paris street riots of 1968 may well have a vividness and a sense of immediacy which a 'better' picture would lack, and this effect will be enhanced by the difficulties of reproducing it. Another way in which reproduction problems are turned to good effect is the trick, beloved of pop artists, of blowing up a newspaper photograph, with its halftone dots monstrously enlarged, in what has now become a cliché-symbol for mass media culture.

But these are the exceptions to the rules, and you must start by knowing the rules themselves. Then, when you want to break them, you can turn to your production team and justify your selection by saying 'Yes, I know it won't reproduce well, but . . .' and giving your reasons. So, what are the rules?

Same size

The fundamental rule is that every picture will lose a little of its quality when it is reproduced. Sometimes the loss will be negligible, as with a clear crude woodcut from the seventeenth century or a Bewick engraving, every blockmaker's dream. The more a picture contains, and the more sophisticated its technique, the more it will lose in reproduction; a painting will lose most of all. This loss of quality will be aggravated if the picture is also reproduced larger or smaller than the original, as we shall note in a moment. Other things being equal (which admittedly they hardly ever are), choose pictures which are to be reproduced more or less the same size ('s/s') as the original.

Enlarging

When pictures are enlarged, they gain in impact and their detail becomes easier to see. If they contain much detail, this may well be all to the good: but if they don't contain enough detail to justify the enlargement, the effect will be to make the picture look empty and ineffectual. So if you're looking for a picture which you know will be used as endpapers in a book, or splashed over two pages or, of course, mounted on a wall in a museum or exhibition, then look for a picture with plenty going on—plenty of action if it's a news scene, plenty of detail if it's an inanimate object.

If you are enlarging a picture which has a halftone screen on it (see 4.07) remember that the pattern of dots which is barely noticeable in the original will become more evident. With rare exceptions, such as those noted above, this should be avoided.

Reducing

Naturally, the opposite is true if you have to reduce. Detail will be lost, elements that are clearly visible in the original will seem to disappear, the whole picture will lose impact. There will be a tendency to fill-in—ink will spread from one line to a close neighbouring line and give a thick, blurred effect; fine lines will either merge or disappear altogether, destroying the artistic finish of the original. This is particularly true of fine steel engravings: those splendid early Victorian topographical views, the kind you see in every local bookshop, in fact reproduce very poorly because it is so difficult to retain the delicacy of the engraved line.

Nevertheless, reduction does not always spoil a picture. Sometimes the original itself was larger than the subject demanded—for instance, when Kate Greenaway was at the height of her fame, her work was sought by such periodicals as the *Graphic*, who were so pleased to have it that they would cover a whole page with her picture, making her usually delicate little drawings seem untypically clumsy.

Reduction gives them back their true character. It is often the case that reducing a picture concentrates it, brings its detail together, helps the reader to focus on it more intensely. For this reason posters, originally intended to be seen from a distance and so deliberately designed on broad bold lines, in the majority of cases reduce satisfactorily when used as book illustrations.

Contrast

All printing processes, as we shall see in the following section, are second bests. The technology of printing has been so skilfully developed that ways have been found to achieve copies that are well nigh perfect—but they remain copies for all that, and the skill required to take advantage of the new technology is not always available. So it is prudent to take as few chances as possible and not make too great a demand on the printer.

A good degree of contrast is always an advantage: good strong blacks and whites, bold patches of colour, rather than delicate shading and subtle hues. However effective the latter may look in the original, there is always the danger that they will be lost in reproduction unless you know your printer is capable of high-quality work.

Bold image

Though not strictly a question of reproduction, this is an appropriate place to recommend looking for pictures with a clear, bold image. When you see pictures in a picture file, you see each one in isolation: when they are reproduced in a book or magazine, they will be competing for attention with other visual material. A single bold image which will reproduce effectively will have greater impact than the softer more delicate picture you might have chosen purely on aesthetic grounds.

Clear colours

Similarly, when you view a transparency on a light box, you see its colours with a brilliancy which no printers' ink can capture. Even the finest Italian separation makers are hamstrung by the necessities of modern high-speed printing. Colour printing has made wonderful advances in the past few decades, but even so it is generally advisable, when you have a choice, to go for the picture where the colours are clearly separated, forming a strong image which stands out clearly.

4.05 The Problems of Reproduction

Most of your problems may be over when you hand over to your editor the pictures you've found, but other peoples' are just beginning. And the way you've done your part will make their problems greater or smaller.

In order to be reproduced, a picture must be in the form of a printing plate or block or the equivalent, which can be inked and brought into contact with paper, over and over again. Some kinds of illustration lend themselves to this more readily than others. A print such as a steel engraving or a woodcut was intended from the start to be reproduced, and so was designed specifically for the printing process: often the original artist also created the actual block or plate used for the printing. When an artist created his work on the block or plate there was, in fact, no 'original'. Almost from the start of photography, too, various standardised mechanical processes were devised to make their reproduction possible (see 4.07).

But other types of illustration, not created with reproduction primarily in mind, call for an additional, intervening process before they can be reproduced. Paintings and drawings, for instance, were originally intended as one-off items to hang on peoples' walls or rest in portfolios. The idea of making them available on a wider scale came later.

Then there is another category, illustrations which for one reason or another *could not* be created in a form suitable for direct reproduction: for example, the sketches of war artists, in pre-camera days: in the heat of battle the reporter had no option but to dash off a hastily drawn impression which could be worked up later by himself or—more usually—by a professional engraver. The same applies to items originally created for one printing method which must subsequently be made suitable for another: for instance, when you want to reproduce a poster or a postage stamp in a book.

The basic problem

The fundamental principle of all printing is that some parts of a given surface are made to leave an impression on a second surface (usually paper) while the other parts do not. The contrast between the two, usually expressed in black and white, creates an image, whether it is a piece of written text or a picture.

With the exception of a few specialised techniques, printing processes cannot handle large unbroken areas of ink: for one thing, surface tension would cause the inked paper to stick to the printing surface and this would slow down the whole process; also the ink would spread and tend to smear, while such heavy inking could make the paper too wet . . . and so on. So the printing surface must be broken up into lines, dots, mottled surfaces or what have you. (After printing, of course, the ink may spread across the paper so as to give the effect of unbroken inking: some processes exploit this effect, others seek to avoid it.)

So all reproduction processes have one thing in common: they require an image made up of lines and/or dots, and if the existing image isn't already so made up, it must be worked on until it is.

If the original is a drawing or an unshaded sketch, there is seldom any serious difficulty. The artist's lines are simply transferred onto the printing block or plate by one of various methods (originally by tracing and transfer, today by a photographic process), and this can usually be achieved without any loss of quality whatever.

But with a more elaborate item such as an oil painting, with all its subtleties of tones and shades, the problem becomes much harder, even without taking colour into account.

Relief or intaglio or flat?

All reproduction processes, old or modern, use one of three basic principles to separate what is to print from what isn't:

- Everything except the desired image is removed, typically by chipping away the unwanted parts from a wooden block. This leaves the image standing clear, in relief, as it were, from the rest, and it is these outstanding parts which are inked and pressed against the paper to print. This is called a *relief process*.
- The image itself is cut away from the surface, typically by gouging down with a cutter into a metal plate. The gouges are then filled with ink from a roller; it is this ink which leaves an impression when pressed against the paper. This is called an *intaglio process*.
- The image is laid on the plate in a material which has different physical or chemical properties from the plate itself: for example, the material may absorb ink while the plate repels it. Then, though the whole plate is inked from a roller, only the image will take up ink and leave an impression when pressed against paper. This is called a *flat* or *planographic process*.

When it comes to printing, there is a further crucial practical difference between these methods. Until recently, almost all books and periodicals were printed by letterpress—that is, a relief process, which gives the best printing of text. This meant that, if illustrations were to be added, the printer had to choose between:

- using only a relief process for the illustrations, so that he could print his type-matter and his illustrations at the same time. But this meant that only very limited types of illustration could be used
- using an intaglio process for the illustrations and the usual relief process for the text, which meant printing the page twice over—awkward and expensive
- printing the illustrations on separate pages from the text, using intaglio for the one and relief for the other, then binding them in together. This too was awkward and expensive, but less so than the second method.

All this explains why, in the majority of books until the last few decades, pictures were printed on separate pages from the text—and still often are when photographic illustrations are being used and the book is not extensively illustrated. The chief exception was the school textbook, where simple line illustrations were generally all that was required and so relief processes could be used. The same applied to low cost illustrated periodicals such as the *Illustrated London News* in pre-photographic days, or *Punch*, which was illustrated exclusively with line illustrations (suitable for relief printing) until well into this century.

But nobody likes having to work within limitations, particularly when they result in either poor quality or high costs. So one of the major concerns of the printing industry has always been to seek better ways of producing illustrated books. How could a way be found to print both text and illustrations by the same process and yet not sacrifice one to the other? The well printed, well produced, heavily illustrated book of today—the kind that most often calls for the picture researcher's services—is the latest stage in a long history of development.

4.06 Older Reproduction Methods

The descriptions which follow have been made as brief and lucid as possible, the purpose being only to speak of each process as it concerns the picture researcher. For fuller accounts see the appropriate books listed in 1.08.

Bear in mind, too, that while we today—particularly art historians with their love of putting all information tidily into pigeonholes—like to label these old prints as 'etchings' or 'woodcuts' or whatever, the people who created them were interested only in the end result and didn't much care by what means they achieved that result. So they used all kinds of variations, and all manner of private tricks of the trade—for example, adding etched lines to aquatints and mezzotints. The art historians have a label even for this, and refer to it as 'mixed style'; but the real truth of the matter is that the old printmakers used whatever techniques came to hand, and even the experts can be fooled by one process doing its damnedest to pass itself off as another. So don't feel too ashamed if you don't always find it easy to spot an aquatint or identify a lithograph!

Woodcut

This was the first way people found to print illustrations. As its name suggests, it is a process whereby the picture was cut on a block of wood, the parts which were not to be inked being cut away to leave only the desired image. It sounds crude, and often was; but in the hands of a really skilled artist like Dürer, astonishing subtlety could be achieved. The process dates from the 14th century, though the oldest surviving example is dated 1423. Most of the earliest illustrated books—Caxton's, for example—used woodcuts until the process of copper engraving emerged. Thereafter the process continued to be used especially where—for the sake of cheapness rather than from any higher motive—it was desired to print text and illustration together, as on public handbills and ballad sheets.

Line engraving: copper

Wood engraving demanded skills which only rare artists possessed. Furthermore, wood blocks soon became worn down with use and lost their first crispness. So it was not long before someone thought of using a metal plate, into which the design was scratched by an engraver. The metal used was generally copper, which is nice and soft: from about 1550 to 1820 copperplate engraving was the dominant form of illustration process. Here again, artists soon learnt to achieve great flexibility in the use of the cutting tool.

In the course of those three centuries many variations were developed. One was a chalk engraving technique, rarely used because of the immense labour involved, but which enabled the engraver to simulate the effect of a chalk drawing so that it is virtually indistinguishable from the original. Another more frequent variation was the stipple engraving, much used towards the end of the 18th century, which used dots rather than lines, jabbed into the copper surface in a way which was partly engraving, partly etching, to give a softer 'feel'.

In all these cases, a plate was produced in which the image was cut in reverse into the metal. When the plate was inked (with a roller) and then wiped, ink remained in the grooves, and under the pressure of the printing press the paper would be forced sufficiently far into the grooves to take up the ink.

Etching

Cutting into metal is hard work. So around 1600 craftsmen began experimenting with a process whereby the metal plate was coated with a softer substance. The cutting was done in this soft 'ground'; after that, acid was poured onto the plate, and where the ground had been cut through the acid bit into the metal plate beneath and cut grooves more or less similar to those the engraver cut with his tools.

Though the original intention was doubtless to save labour, what made the etching popular with artists—who have never been shy of hard work to achieve their effects—was that, because they were cutting into a softer material, they could achieve much more flexible lines. The result is easy to see: etchings tend to be subtler, gentler, more personal, more spontaneous. For this reason, the etching has retained its popularity with artists, whereas engraving has been superseded by other processes. It was used by many of the great artists—Hollar in the 17th century, Gillray at the end of the 18th, George Cruikshank in the 19th—and offered a useful alternative to engraving throughout the period 1600 to 1850.

Mezzotint

All the techniques hitherto evolved relied on lines or, in some cases, dots and stippling. None could do more than give a crude indication of shading. There was an understandable desire among illustrators to find a process which would come closer to reproducing the continuous shading of an oil painting: the mezzotint, developed around the middle of the 17th century, was the answer.

It was immensely hard work to produce. First the metal plate had to be roughened all over by rocking a serrated tool over the plate which, if finely worked, would have as many as 250,000 indentations to the square inch! Then this burr was scraped away, to a greater or lesser degree depending on whether the area was to be light or dark: the more it was scraped, the less ink it would hold, the lighter it would print.

The effects were magnificent, often works of art in their own right. The technique is characteristically associated with portraits of under-dressed ladies of the Restoration court, but was used throughout the 18th century and well into the 19th for portraits and other high-class work. Though it originated in Holland, it was so popular in aristocratic England that it became known as *la manière anglaise*. But the inordinate amount of work involved prevented it becoming truly popular, despite the fact that it was the only reproduction process then available to offer continuous tone.

Aquatint

The aquatint was invented towards the close of the 18th century, coinciding with the boom in water-colour painting whose delicate effects it was designed to simulate and reproduce: hence its name. Just as the mezzotint was devised to introduce shading into engraving, so the aquatint sought to introduce shading into etching.

Whereas the etching plate had a smooth surface, the aquatint plate had a roughened one, a prepared coating which, if printed without working, would give an overall mottled finish. This was scraped away by the etcher to a greater or lesser degree according to the tone he wanted. By carrying out these operations several times, biting out with acid each time, many different degrees of shade could be achieved: etched lines were added to provide outlines if required.

The aquatint's characteristic stipple effect is more clearly marked than the soft burr of the mezzotint, and the areas of shade have clearly defined edges because the shade is achieved in a series of succeeding stages, not by infinitely gradual working.

The vogue of the aquatint was not long, roughly 1790 to 1820: its expiry was due partly to the labour involved, partly to the invention of lithography which to a large extent improved on it. But during that time some wonderful results were achieved, and no other process was ever able to simulate so effectively the soft delicacy of water-colour painting.

Lithograph

Developed at about the same time as the aquatint, the lithograph was slow to gain popularity, but when it did it retained it permanently and is still widely used by artists today. No other process so effectively captures the feeling of an original drawing: indeed, it is often well nigh impossible to distinguish a good lithograph from a drawing except by physical or chemical testing.

In the lithograph the original drawing is conveyed onto a block— originally of stone, hence the name (*lithos* is Greek for stone). This transfer was done in various ways, but the crucial factor was the use of a greasy substance capable of being absorbed by the stone. When the stone is dampened, water is retained by all except the greasy image; then, when the stone is inked, the wet parts repel the ink while the greasy parts retain it and transfer it to the paper under pressure.

Lithographs were widely used throughout the nineteenth century. Perhaps the most probable form in which you are likely to come across them is in those magnificent portfolios of scenes from the various imperial battlefronts—the Afghan Wars, the Crimea, the Indian Mutiny—where the glorious achievements of the British fighting man were magnificently captured in a graphic splendour no other process could match.

Steel engraving

Basically, the steel engraving was much the same as the copper engraving, except that the basic metal was harder. The primary consideration, no doubt, was to give the printer a plate he could use more often before it started to wear out: but in so doing a side-effect was discovered. Engraving on steel gave a completely different feel to the print, due to the hardness of the metal and therefore to the narrowness of the lines the plate would hold. This effect was increased when the plate was inked, as in the harder metal the ink tended to spread less and so retained the delicacy of the incised line.

The characteristics were put to superb use by a school of engravers, most of them British, during the period from about 1825 to 1865: familiar are the volumes of topographical prints produced by Bartlett, Allom, Shepherd and others. Enormously popular then as now, these are the characteristic engraved views still to be seen, at ever climbing prices, in the windows of print shops, neatly enclosed in their black and gold Hogarth frames.

Unfortunately, while the originals are often wonderful, they are far from easy to reproduce. Few printing processes can cope satisfactorily with those fine lines and that subtle detail, and you should be very careful indeed when using them. If they are to be enlarged there is usually no serious problem; but use of them s/s or reduced nearly always results in filling-in, coarsening of line and loss of detail, sadly reducing the effect for which you chose the picture in the first place.

Wood engraving

By far the most widely used reproduction method, among these older processes, was the wood engraving, which was introduced in the early years of the 19th century to meet the demand for cheaper books and illustrated periodicals.

The wood engraving is a modification of the woodcut: the differences are technical, starting with the fact that, while in the woodcut the soft side-grain of the wood had been used, in the wood engraving it was the harder end grain. This was tougher—and tougher on the artist—but it meant that the wood could be truly engraved, not simply cut, enabling more detail to be captured and greater subtlety achieved. The printer benefited, too, because he could run off many more copies before his block started to deteriorate.

The wood engraving meant that text and illustrations could be printed together on the same page at the same time, for the first time since the old woodcuts with which illustration processes had begun. Printing costs were dramatically reduced, making it possible to publish cheap illustrated books for the mass market, illustrated textbooks, and above all the illustrated periodical. Before long the vast majority of illustration was being produced by this process: the *Illustrated London News* and its many rivals all used wood engraving or later modifications of it.

As a result, engraving became a highly organised trade employing vast numbers of craftsmen to work the blocks. The original drawing—perhaps an artist's sketch by a reporter at the scene of a riot or battle—was transferred onto the wood block and then cut away by the engraver. When big blocks had to be made in a hurry, such as a whole-page picture for the *Illustrated London News*, the block would be made up of several smaller segments, each of which would be cut by an individual engraver. They would then be married together and a master craftsmen would do his best to conceal the joins by adding further engraving where necessary.

As the 19th century progressed, ways were found to streamline and speed the process. First, it was found possible to transfer the original image directly onto the block by photographic means. Then the wood block was replaced by a metal one, and the photographic image was etched onto the metal block by a mechanical process, known as *photo-engraving* or *process engraving*. The image was photographed onto a zinc plate which was exposed to acid which cut it away everywhere except where the image was.

These technical improvements were more or less standard from the 1870s on, and by the end of the century the wood block as such was obsolete. It is virtually impossible, however, to distinguish between a process engraving produced mechanically and a 'true' wood engraving. But the high standards of reproduction quality—if not always of aesthetic quality—noticeable in end-of-the-century printing are the consequence of this development, though it was deplored at the time because it seemed to take creativity entirely out of the business.

Identifying old reproduction techniques

Only experience can teach you to distinguish one technique from another, and even years of experience will not make you infallible. These rule-of-thumb tests are intended only as guidelines:

Picture made up only of lines often, though not necessarily always, rather crude; printed on same page as text.	Woodcut or wood engraving. (The differences between the two are discernible, though not always, to the expert, but are not of sufficient importance to the researcher to make it worth while going into detail.)

Illustration printed on separate page from text.	Almost certainly one of the intaglio processes.
Fine, hard, close-packed lines, tending to be somewhat stiff and formal, but with great subtlety in such items as clouds or trees.	Steel engraving.
As above, but softer, seldom attempting to reproduce cloud or other subtle effects.	Copper engraving.
As above, but with free-flowing lines which look as if 'done by hand'.	Etching
Mottled effect in tone areas, often with clear lines as well.	Aquatint
Seemingly unbroken areas of tone, shading into one another: few or no hard lines, overall sombre effect, heavy dark areas.	Mezzotint
Soft effect as if done by crayon, sometimes with harder lines added.	Lithograph

Colour

Although it was generally accepted that illustration must be in black and white, there was always a desire on the part of publishers to offer their public pictures in colour. Hand colouring of black-and-white prints dates from very early, though it is generally impossible without chemical tests to be sure whether the hand colouring is contemporary or added later.

Until about 1800 such colouring remained rare: one suspects it was often a case of individuals colouring up their own prints. But towards the end of the eighteenth century there was a great outburst of popular political prints, done by Gillray, Rowlandson and others, and publishers found it worth their while to get these coloured so that they could charge half a crown for a print that sold for a shilling uncoloured. Sometimes the colour was laid over large areas by the use of stencils placed over defined areas, but for the most part the colourists had no aids. Those wonderful coloured-plate books which today fetch such fancy prices—Ackermann's Repository, the Rowlandson and Pugin topographical series—were produced on an assembly-line basis, rows of colourists adding the colours one at a time. For this reason, examination will show that no two are precisely alike—for all their skill, there are minute differences every time.

Some print techniques lent themselves to the addition of a second *printed* colour without great difficulty; for instance, you will often see lithographs from around 1840 with a second colour, usually a sandy beige, which without giving the effect of a fully coloured picture certainly enhances the print. Aquatints, too, had additional blocks of colour added in much the same way. Because this practice meant printing the plate a second time, with the problem of ensuring that the second printing lined up perfectly with the first, it was never standard practice except for the more expensive type of print.

From this, it was a natural step to developing ways of producing *colour* prints, as opposed to *coloured* prints. Colour printing, properly so-called, was not really achieved until the 1830s, and even then was reserved only for a very few expensive books aimed at the quality market. There were several competing processes, but all involved using multiple blocks, each block involving a separate printing operation.

Each printer developed his own methods, sometimes amounting to a distinct process: these were jealously guarded secrets which sometimes accompanied their inventor to the grave. Today, in many cases, experts can only speculate as to the means whereby some of the colour printing was achieved. Baxter, one of the most famous colour printers in Victorian England, is known to have run some of his prints through the press as many as twenty times to get the subtlety of colour for which he was celebrated.

Colour printing from woodblocks, combined with black-and-white wood engravings, was the popular equivalent of these quality efforts. The results can be seen in Christmas numbers of the *Illustrated London News* and *Graphic* from the 1860s on. The earlier attempts were fairly crude—slabs of simple colour laid on with little subtlety. The biggest breakthrough in the popular field came with the development of the late Victorian children's book, with illustrations by Greenaway, Thomas Crane, M. Ellen Edwards and countless others—printed in colour throughout, the vivid colour made possible by the most Victorian of printing processes, the chromolithograph.

Soon the process was being used for all kinds of popular printing, including greetings cards and postcards as well as books of various kinds. Various techniques were used, and it is not necessary to explore them in detail. But you can be fairly confident that while before 1840 all colour was applied by hand, after 1860 virtually none was: between those two dates it is an open question.

Dating prints by their processing

When you know by what process a print was made, you are well on the way to being able to estimate its date. The table which follows gives only a crude time-scale for each process: however, even apart from internal clues such as fashion changes, there were developments in technique which, when you get to know them, will enable you to narrow the date much more precisely. But these dates give you at least a starting point:

Woodcut	1450–1600
Woodcut, used in ballad or popular broadsheet	Any time to 1850
Copper engraving	1550–1825
Etching	Any time from 1600
Mezzotint	1650–1850, but mostly 18th century
Aquatint	1790–1820
Lithograph	From 1780 but mostly after 1830
Steel engraving	1825–1860
Wood engraving (and later process engraving)	1800–1900
Hand-coloured prints	mostly 1780–1850
Colour prints	From 1840

4.07 Modern Reproduction Methods

It is helpful to know by what process your book is going to be printed, because certain types of illustration are better suited to one process than to another. True, modern printing is so good that such considerations are not so crucial as formerly; nevertheless there are some factors which should be kept in mind, and a knowledge of what each process entails will help you make your selection.

Each of the three major printing processes in use today can be seen as a sophisticated version of one or other of the methods described in the preceding section:

- the woodblock led to the halftone used in *letterpress*
- the line engraving led to *gravure*
- the lithograph led to *offset*.

Letterpress

Ever since the invention of printing, this has been the preferred process for printing typematter, the text of a book. It is the familiar process whereby letters, all of a standard height, are held together in a chase, inked, then pressed onto the paper. Illustrations could be combined with typematter, as we have seen, if they were in the form of relief blocks. Other types of illustration, especially those with areas of tone, being unsuitable for relief blocks, had to be printed by some other process.

Until the latter half of the nineteenth century, this situation was acceptable: readers who could afford it purchased books in which the illustrations, in the form of engravings or lithographs, were printed separately from the text, while others made do with line blocks. But the invention of photography brought things to a crisis, for the general public demanded photographic illustrations. But how could they be provided at a reasonable cost? To start with, photographic illustrations were printed separately and the pages inserted, as with the engravings and lithographs, but this was clearly too costly. So somehow a method had to be found to incorporate photographic illustration with letterpress, which remained the only method of printing the text.

A temporary expedient was found, whereby photographs were laboriously 'translated' into line blocks by engravers. You will often see, in periodicals published between 1860 and 1890, line engravings which betray their photographic origins by the 'natural' way people are standing or perspective is depicted. The skill with which this was done, especially by American engravers, was astonishing: the results could never be mistaken for photographs, but they retained a good deal of the photograph's authenticity. But for all their virtuosity, they were none the less a compromise: all kinds of experimentation went on to find a mechanical way of turning photographs into something that could be printed in the text.

The eventual result was the halftone, which must surely rank as one of the great breakthroughs in communications history. In this method, the photograph is copied through a very fine screen, so that the image is broken down into a vast number of tiny dots, more or less invisible to the naked eye, on a metal plate. By a chemical process the plate is next bitten away except where the dots are, thus leaving a relief block made of dots. They are denser where the photograph was dark, less dense where it was light. The fineness of the screen determines the subtlety with which the original image is reproduced. The finer the better, of course, but the paper used for cheaper publications isn't capable of holding a fine-screen halftone without the narrow space between the dots filling in and blurring. So a popular newspaper will use a screen of from 55 to 100 dots to the inch, whereas a glossy magazine like *Vogue* is likely to have 150.

When used well, aided by a conscientious blockmaker and a skilful printer, the halftone process can produce splendid results with remarkably little loss of detail. But it can also be used appallingly, and the dreadful quality of newspapers and periodicals during the first three decades of the twentieth century remain to show what horrors it could produce—perhaps the lowest point in the history of printing.

Since then things have grown a lot better. But in the meantime ways have been found of printing typematter effectively by other processes. Letterpress, for hundreds of years the 'normal' way of producing books, is increasingly obsolescent thanks to recent developments in offset litho, as we shall see shortly.

But, though fewer illustrations are being reproduced by the halftone process, this is still the form in which a great number of pictures exist, and they present an awkward problem for the printer, and therefore for the researcher. You should be wary of offering, for use in a publication to be printed by letterpress, a picture which has *already* been given a halftone screen—that is, one which has already been printed somewhere else. When printed a second time, a new screen will be laid over the original screen: this may not only result in a further loss of detail, but also sometimes leads to a psychedelic patterning effect arising from the overlay of the two screen patterns, completely spoiling the picture. This can usually be avoided if the picture is re-printed using a different screen from the original, and/ or to a different size. But printers are understandably reluctant to accept pictures which already have a screen, and they should not be chosen if unscreened pictures are to be had.

Gravure (photogravure and rotogravure)

This process can be seen as deriving from the engraving, in that the areas which hold the ink are cut into the surface instead of standing out above it. It is more or less the contrary of the halftone, a series of pits being cut into the plate by a mechanical screening method similar to that which produces halftone dots. The picture is thus converted into pits whose varying depths, holding more or less ink, create darker or lighter shades when printed.

The gravure process gives finer shading than the halftone: 150 dots to the inch is normal, not exceptional, so that even a piece of mediocre gravure printing can match the best halftones in fineness of detail and subtlety of shading. It is often virtually impossible to discern the fine white lines left by the ridges of the pits, due to the spreading of the ink from one pit to the next. This effect is of course welcomed by the printer. Though detail is in fact being lost between one pit and its neighbour, the size is so small that it hardly matters.

Because its tones are achieved by using more or less ink, not by greater or lesser density of pits, gravure can achieve a higher degree of contrast than the halftone. Where gravure is distinctly less satisfactory, apart from its expense, is when it comes to the typematter: there is always a vague smudginess about the text in publications printed by gravure, which explains why it is rarely used for books but chiefly for popular illustrated magazines.

From the researcher's point of view, much the same considerations apply to gravure as to letterpress, though, because of the spreading effect, the consequence of previous screening is not so noticeable, and printing pictures which were originally gravure by letterpress is not a serious problem.

Gravure is sometimes known as rotogravure, referring to the fact that it is carried out on a rotary machine for mass production of large-circulation periodicals.

Offset litho

This is a sophisticated development from lithography, in which the type (set on film) and illustrations are printed on a litho plate, and thence on to paper. It enables very fine screens to be used—up to 300 dots to the inch—so that litho printing is far superior to its rivals when it comes to giving the illusion of continuous tone without loss of detail.

Against this is the drawback that offset litho sometimes tends to give a rather neutral overall look to pictures, losing contrast and vividness and resulting in a flattish effect which misses both the precise impression of letterpress or the high contrast of gravure. However, great strides are being made in the development of offset litho, and quality is improving very rapidly: at the same time its cost advantages and ease of handling encourage its use on a wide range of applications. It seems well nigh certain that this will be the preferred printing process for illustrated books of almost every kind: already probably a majority of the books for which you are researching will be printed by this method.

This means that you have a greater freedom of choice than the older processes give you. Virtually anything can be effectively reproduced by litho: though there will still be a certain loss of quality when a previously screened photograph is used for the second time, the loss will not be serious. Consequently almost any kind of original artwork can be used: you may safely offer postcards, magazine illustrations, cigarette cards, printed ephemera of all kinds, as well as newspaper photos where the original has been lost.

What you *should* look for, though, is a highly contrasty picture which will give a strong bold image. A highly detailed and subtle steel engraving, for instance, will tend to lose a good deal of its original quality when printed by litho.

Silk screen

You may occasionally be asked to research pictures for silk screen printing, so you may as well know what it is. Although not practicable for book or magazine printing, silk screen gives excellent results for one-off prints, such as posters, and has a lot of potential. It is basically a kind of mechanical stencil. Ink is forced through unmasked areas of a mesh—originally of silk, today of very fine wire or nylon or similar plastic—onto the paper, where it spreads again and so creates an overall area of colour which gives strong solid effects. It is slow and relatively costly, but gives very striking results, and may well come to have wider applications when it has been further developed.

Collotype

Although little used in Britain because it is expensive and demands great skill from the printer, collotype is the only commercial printing process which gives a true continuous tone. When originally developed in the 1870s, it used a gummy substance called collodion, hence the name: this was later replaced by an emulsion of bichromated gelatin which is equally sensitive to light. The image is transferred onto the printing plate by putting light through the negative, which hardens the chemical on the plate to a greater or lesser degree, making it less or more water absorbent and consequently more or less ready to hold ink. The actual process is then much like lithography.

Since it requires no screening, a very high quality of reproduction can be achieved. Separations can be made for colour printing, and very precise reproductions of the original colour can be achieved because the process does not rely on the trichromatic system (see below) but adds each colour as a true colour. The results are generally acknowledged to be superior to any other form of colour printing, but it demands not only time but very great skill, and is therefore used only for very high quality work which justifies the outlay.

Colour printing

All the processes described above lend themselves to colour printing, using additional blocks or plates for each additional colour. In all except collotype, colour is achieved not by making a separate plate for each of the colours which will eventually be discernible, but for the three primary colours of which all other colours are composed—red, yellow and blue. In practice a fourth plate—black—is usually added to give greater depth. As you can imagine, the preparation of these plates—known as 'separations'—is an astonishingly intricate business, demanding skilful control both when the original colours are broken up into their component elements and when they are recombined on the printed page. This, together with the fact that each plate requires a separate printing process, explains why colour printing is so very much more expensive than monochrome.

4.08 Photographic Techniques

Here is another specialised field in which nobody expects the picture researcher to be an expert, but where a smattering of knowledge will help you to avoid some of the more blatant pitfalls. It is important, clearly, to know in what historical periods it is reasonable to expect to find photographs, and when you must resign yourself to artwork of some kind—are there photographs of Stephenson's 'Rocket' in action? Lord Palmerston? Shelley? Building the Crystal Palace? (Answers: no, yes, no, yes.) So it's important to get the history of photography into perspective, and then to see how modern developments affect your job.

The historical development of photography

The first photographs were taken in France during the 1820s, but for more than a decade photography was an experimental affair, and the few surviving photographs from this period, though fascinating to students of the subject, are of little intrinsic significance and certainly offer no alternative to artwork as regards documentation.

Then, from about 1840, photography advanced rapidly. First, for portraits. Everyone was curious to know what they 'really' looked like, and even in those early days photographs were a lot cheaper than having your portrait painted. It also offered a means whereby everyone could own a pictorial souvenir of a political or military hero, a favourite actress or dancer, or Our Own Beloved Queen. Newcomers to the subject are sometimes surprised to discover that high-quality photographic portraits exist of most of the eminent Victorians, if only in the form of *carte-de-visite* photographs, a little larger than the visiting cards after which they are named, which were sold in vast quantities just as prints had been in earlier decades.

Some topographical photographs also exist from the early years of photography. The detail is often superb, though they suffer from a lack of animation due to the fact that exposures were still so long that any moving object, if it shows up in the photograph at all, does so in the form of a shadowy blur.

The first really important photographic documentation is probably that which Roger Fenton and others made of the Crimean War (1854–55). Considering their cumbersome equipment and the other technical obstacles, these photographers produced marvellous results, but of course their subject-matter was necessarily limited to static subjects. There are no photographs of the Charge of the Light Brigade: for that, you must turn to the engravings in the *Illustrated London News* and the lithographs of the souvenir albums made from sketches made on the spot by intrepid artist-reporters.

Things hadn't changed much by the time the American Civil War broke out in the following decade: Brady's memorable camp scenes and military portraits must still be supplemented with drawings and engravings. But the photographer was gradually moving into such areas of the documentation field as could be recorded at leisure: from this period come the first genre subjects—views of slums, seaside scenes, fishermen at work. The well known figures of street characters which appear in Mayhew's *London Labour and London Poor* in the 1860s, though known to us in their engraved form, were taken from on-the-spot photographs.

As the century progressed, the range of material gradually widened. But cameras were still unwieldy tools, and the job of processing the pictures they took was still a laborious one, so right up to the 1880s it was rare to get action pictures of current events. When Eadweard Muybridge produced his celebrated studies of the human figure and animals in motion, the camera was for the first time able to do what neither the human eye nor the artist's pencil had ever been able to do—to seize movement and freeze it for ever more.

In the 1890s came roll film, smaller and lighter cameras, easier processing. Matching these developments came the halftone block (see 4.07) which made possible the reproduction of photographs in printed publications without tedious hand engraving. These early reproductions were for the most part of an appalling standard, but such was the public demand for realism that the process was almost universally adopted. Cheap popular magazines, illustrated throughout with halftones, consisted of page after page of shadowy smudges: but at their best—see for instance the *Tatler* around the year 1904—reproduction was magnificent and wholly justified the changeover to the new process. From this time on, photographic illustration was the norm, though the public had reluctantly to accept that it couldn't expect a photograph of the midnight sinking of the *Titanic* . . .

Photographs and artwork continued side by side until after World War I, but the awareness of the camera's unique potential for reportage urged on development. From the 1920s on, it was taken for granted that nobody would do anything important without making sure there was somebody on hand with a camera to record it: saturation reportage had arrived.

Recording of everyday life was more haphazard. The possibilities of the camera as a way of 'fixing' the social scene, foreshadowed by Mayhew, were well appreciated in George Sims' epoch-making *Living London*, issued by Newnes as a partwork between 1900 and 1903, detailing—almost entirely by means of photographs—all kinds of everyday scenes, from dinner in a boarding house to 'a move in slumopolis'. This unacknowledged landmark in the history of photo-reportage has never been matched since: it remains a unique effort, fixing a particular era in a way that no other period has ever been recorded. Apart from Sims' work, it is for the most part a hit or miss matter if you set out to find a photograph of, say, an Edwardian picnic, or a housewife of the 1920s doing her shopping. Such photographs may well exist, but tracking them down is likely to be a long and tiresome business.

But at least, from the 1920s on, there is a possibility that you may find a photograph of almost anything imaginable, from children paddling at Skegness to the footprints of the Abominable Snowman (Eric Shipton, 1951). And the range of material has broadened to include aerial photography, microphotography, high-speed photography, underwater photography, astrophotography, infrared photography . . .

Copying old photographs

One of the great secondary advantages of the photograph is that it can be so easily copied. If the original negative exists, a perfect print can be made over and over again with a minimum of trouble. Even if the negative has been lost or destroyed, as is true of the majority of historical photographs, it is generally possible to re-photograph the print with virtually no loss of quality. Indeed, many old prints are actually improved by being copied, as in the process it is possible to restore the original strength and contrast which have been lost by fading.

Modern photographic collections

Most collections of modern material consist, inevitably, almost entirely of photographs, either black-and-white or colour or both.

Black-and-white material

This is usually in the form of 25 × 20 cm (10 × 8 in) or more rarely 15 × 20 cm (6 × 8 in) glossy prints. Typically, a black-and-white photo library will keep a negative file and a print file in separate parts of the establishment: each print will carry the negative number. Practice varies as to whether they let you take away their filed prints, or require you to order a further copyprint by quoting the negative number on the file or contact print.

Colour material

This is nearly always in the form of transparencies, sometimes referred to as ektachromes. A transparency, unlike a black-and-white print, is the photograph itself as the photographer took it, without necessitating a further process: except for the basic cost of the materials, therefore, it is much easier to use and handle. It is also usually much smaller: many photo libraries house enormous numbers of photographs in a few unimpressive filing cabinets.

As regards the preferred transparency size, practice varies. Most commercial sources are made up chiefly of 35mm, which is the size taken by most photographers on normal reportage work. The quality is usually adequate for all normal reproduction purposes. Some editors and designers like to work from larger formats, but the size is dictated ultimately by the eventual size at which the picture is to be reproduced. If a 35mm picture is enlarged overmuch—say, for the purposes of making a poster—it may lose some or much of its quality.

Photographers working in studios are not so wedded to the compact camera, with the result that they are readier to supply larger transparencies. Fine art photographers in particular are apt to use 12 × 9cm (5 × 4in) or even larger: the *National Portrait Gallery* is not alone in prohibiting the use of 35mm and requiring transparencies of at least 5 × 5in. Many photographers feel that this is a nuisance; and certainly the awkwardness of handling large format transparencies, so easily bent or damaged, is a factor against using them. The *Mary Evans Picture Library* has opted for an in-between size of 9 × 6cm (4 × 2½in) which is substantially larger than 35mm but escapes the vulnerability of the larger sizes. As we said earlier, practice varies!

Transparencies can be copied by simply making a duplicate. In expert hands, the loss of quality will be negligible, but in the present state of technology it isn't easy to ensure perfect colour control, so that 'dupes' are always looked upon with suspicion both by the client, who wants the best material available, and by the photographer, who wants his work to appear at its best. It is in fact cheaper and easier for the photographer to bang off several identical or near-identical photographs of a subject for which there is likely to be a big demand.

Ownership of photographs

As you will have discovered if you read the section 2.12 on copyright, the question of who owns a photograph is anything but simple. So complex is it, and at the same time so important, that we make no apology for recapping here some of the issues as they affect the researcher:

- If you take or make a photograph, you own that photograph and the copyright in it, and can do what you like with it.
- If you pay someone to take a photograph, you own the copyright

and can reproduce it wherever and whenever you wish. But it will be the photographer who owns the negative (though he may not reproduce from it without your permission) unless he sells it to you or it is stipulated on your order to him that you will own the negative.

● If the photographer is an employee of a publishing house, it may be stipulated in his contract that the pictures he takes for the company are wholly the company's—negatives, copyright and all.

● If you photograph, or commission someone else to photograph, something that is itself in copyright, you own the copyright of the *photograph*, but the copyright of the *original item* remains with its original owner.

● If you photograph, or commission someone else to photograph, something which, though out of copyright, is in someone else's possession, you have copyright in your photograph, so that nobody else can use it, unless you give them permission, but neither can you reproduce it until you yourself have obtained permission from the owner of the original item (nor, of course can you stop anyone else using *their* photo of that item unless you have specifically been granted exclusive rights).

So, if you want to reproduce a photograph taken by a freelance photographer for a publisher of a painting by a recently deceased artist which has been purchased by a certain museum, you must make sure that you obtain permission from the photographer, the publisher, the artist's heirs and the museum before you can feel free to go ahead . . .

. . . are you still sure you want to be a picture researcher?

GLOSSARY

This section contains brief definitions of words and phrases often described more fully in the main part of the book. The figures in brackets refer to the section of the book where more complete information is to be found. These are not dictionary definitions, but working explanations, phrased with the picture researcher's specialist needs in mind.

Access fee   Fee charged by museums and galleries for the facility of photographing items in their collections. Also known as facility fee. (2.10)

ADAGP   French association for protecting the copyright of graphic works. (1.07)

Advice note   (= Delivery Note) Document accompanying a consignment of pictures sent to client by picture source, containing details of numbers and subjects and often specifying conditions. It may have a returnable counterfoil for you to send back indicating that you have received the material and that you accept their conditions of business. (3.09)

AFAEP   Association of Fashion, Advertising and Editorial Photographers. (1.07)

Agency/Agent   Picture source handling the work of several artists or photographers on a commission or shared-profits basis. (2.04)

Agency fee   Share of the reproduction fee taken by agency handling work of artist or photographer. (2.04)

ALA   Associate of the Library Association. (1.07)

ANDRPC   French photo source association. (1.07)

Aquatint   Type of print using 'mottled' areas to resemble watercolour painting. (4.06)

ARLIS   The Art Libraries Society, a British organisation with international affiliations. (1.07)

Artist's Copy   Copy of an existing picture, reproducing the original in sufficient detail to be recognisable, but modifying it for the sake of either simplicity or uniformity of style. (see Rates 2.11)

Artwork   The illustration (whether originally a photograph, drawing or whatever) in the form in which it is used by the printer. While most pictures themselves constitute artwork, exceptions occur when intermediate stages are required: for instance, the Mona Lisa on the wall of the Louvre is not artwork in this sense, whereas a photograph or engraving of it is.

ASMP   An American association of photographers, now calling themselves 'The Society of Photographers in Communications Inc'. (1.07)

ASPP   American Society of Picture Professionals. (1.07)

BAPLA   The British Association of Picture Libraries and Agencies. (1.07)

Block   (originally) The piece of wood into which a woodcut or wood engraving is cut: later replaced by metal. (4.06)

(subsequently) The piece of metal to which a picture is photographically transferred for halftone printing. (4.07)

Blocking fee   (=Holding Fee) Fee charged when pictures are retained beyond a specified period, thus 'blocking' them from use by others. (2.10)

Bromide   A photographic copyprint, so called because the paper used is coated with silver bromide.

Budget   Money allowed for an assignment by a publisher. It may cover reproduction fees only, or include researcher's remuneration, expenses, holding fees, print fees, etc. (3.04)

Chromolithograph   ('Chromo') Colour print made by a process derived from lithography, used in the late 19th century and conspicuous by its vivid and lasting colours. (4.06)

Circulation   Number of copies printed by a periodical or other publication. Usually averaged over a six-month period.

Collotype   A flat printing process used for high quality art reproduction. (4.07)

Colour library   Picture source whose material consists only of colour material, generally in the form of transparencies. (4.08)

Colour print   (1) Printed picture in which the colour is reproduced mechanically, usually by separate blocks. (4.06, 4.07)

(2) Print of a colour photograph made from negative.

Coloured print   Picture in which colour is added to the print by hand. Particularly applied to coloured engravings of the early 19th century. (4.06)

Conditions   (1) Terms on which a picture source allows its material to be borrowed and used. (2.09)

(2) Conditions of employment either as staff or freelance.

Copyprint   Print taken from a photographic negative.

Copynegative   Duplicate negative, or negative made from a photographic print, usually because the original negative has been lost.

Copyright   The right to copy, or authorise the copying of, a picture. (2.12)

Courtesy copyright   An acknowledgement, not legally required but ethically desirable, to owners of out-of-copyright material. (2.12)

CPNA   Council of Photographic and News Agencies. (1.07)

Credit   Printed indication in a publication of the source from which an illustration was obtained. (3.12)

Delivery note   = Advice Note.

Dia (positive)   Print of a colour photo made from negative.

Dry mounting   Method of mounting picture on card, etc., by placing a sheet of adhesive material between picture and mount, which melts when they are placed in a heated press and forms a permanent bond.

Dummy   Sample presentation of a proposed publication, usually in the form of a few typical pages, intended to show potential publishers or advertisers what the finished publication will be like. Sometimes printed, sometimes put together by hand. (Rates, 2.11)

Dupe   = Duplicate, generally of a transparency. (4.08)

Edition   'The whole number of copies printed from the same set of types and issued at one time' says the Shorter Oxford Dictionary, but in practice it isn't so simple. So see 2.11.

Engraving   Form of print created by cutting the image into a metal plate, or cutting away all except the image from a wood block. (4.06)

Ektachrome   Alternative name for a transparency, derived from a particular brand name.

Etching   Form of print created by cutting the image into a specially coated plate, the image then being cut into the plate through the exposed parts by acid treatment. (4.06)

Exclusive right   Right granted to a client to use an illustration with the guarantee that no other client in the same sphere of activity and/ or geographical region will be allowed to use that picture within a specified period. (3.11)

Facility fee   = Access Fee.

Fairs, Book   Commercial exhibitions, held (usually annually) in various business centres, where new publications or projects are displayed to the book trade for the purpose of selling books or rights. (1.02)

Flash   Single showing of a picture on television. (Rates 2.11)

Foreign language rights   Rates 2.11, Rights 3.11

Frankfurt   The Frankfurt Book Fair, held annually in September/ October, where publishers from all over the world display their wares. Some picture sources also exhibit. (1.02)

Gravure   (= photogravure, rotogravure) Intaglio printing process for which illustrations are prepared by screening and indenting the plate with 'pits' of varying depths to give different tones. (4.07)

Halftone   Relief printing process for which illustrations are prepared by being screened to form dots of varying density on the printing block. Also, the block itself. (4.07)

Holding fee   (= blocking fee) Fee charged by picture sources when pictures are retained by a client beyond a specified period. (2.10)

IIP   Institute of Incorporated Photographers. (1.07)

Intaglio   Printing processes in which the ink is held below the surface level of the plate, in grooves or pits, into which the paper is pressed to take up the ink and so transfer the image. (4.06, 4.07)

Interim service fee   Fee charged by some picture sources on long-term projects, as part-payment of service costs incurred in early stages. (2.10)

Layout   (1) The way in which illustrations and type-matter are arranged on the page for printing.

(2) A designer's preliminary designs for a printed publication.

Letterpress   Relief printing process designed primarily for the printing of type-matter. If they are to be used with letterpress printing, illustrations must be in the form of a line or halftone block according to the nature of the original artwork. (4.06, 4.07)

Library Association   (1.07)

Line block   Printing block made from artwork composed only of lines, therefore requiring no screen to make it suitable for printing. (4.06, 4.07)

Line engraving   A print in which the image is created with lines, without areas of tone: most frequent are woodcut, wood engraving, copper plate, steel engraving. (4.06)

Lithograph   Flat surface reproduction process in which (originally) the illustration was printed from a stone block to which the image had been transferred in non-water-absorbent material. (4.06)

Litho printing   Modern flat-surface printing process derived from lithography. (4.07)

Mask   Cover used to hide unwanted or indicate wanted sections of an illustration when only certain parts of it are to be reproduced. Usually made of transparent paper so that the designer's intentions can be clearly seen.

Mezzotint   Form of print created by removing a roughened surface to a greater or lesser degree from a metal plate thus creating areas of continuous tone: used to simulate the effect of painting. (4.06)

Museums Association   (1.07)

Network   Broadcast over an entire television system, as opposed to 'local', 'regional' or 'originating area only'.

Non-theatrical rights   Permission to broadcast an illustration on television, but not when the programme is shown in a theatre or similar venue. (3.11)

NUJ   National Union of Journalists. (1.07)

Offset litho (= photo-offset lithography) Modern flat-surface printing process derived from the principles of lithography. (4.07)

Open access System whereby a picture source or library permits researchers direct access to material.

Originating area Local television broadcasting region, as opposed to network.

Partwork A publication which appears in sections and over a period of time, though usually building up to form a complete work with a defined end. Unlike a periodical, it contains no advertising.

Photocopy An ambiguous and therefore to-be-avoided word used sometimes to designate a photostat, sometimes a copyprint.

Photo engraving Process whereby a picture is mechanically transferred to a line block, or through a screen to a halftone block, to make it suitable for letterpress printing. (4.06, 4.07)

Photogravure = Gravure.

Photostat Low-cost copy of a picture made by xerography or some equivalent process, giving a limited-quality copy suitable for reference but not usually adequate for reproduction. (3.08)

Planographic printing 'Flat' printing processes, as opposed to intaglio or relief. Includes the lithograph and the collotype. (4.06, 4.07)

Plate (1) In printing, the piece of metal to which illustrations and type-matter are transferred for gravure or litho printing. (4.07)
(2) in photography, a sensitised glass plate used before the invention of the roll film.
(3) Photographic prints are still sometimes measured in pre-metric plate sizes—such as 'whole plate', 'half plate' etc., related to the glass plates referred to in (2) above.
(4) An illustration in a book.

Polaroid System of 'instant' photography enabling pictures to be copied photographically to reproduction standard, with prints available in a few seconds. (3.08)

Press agency Picture source whose material relates primarily to current events and newsworthy personalities. Almost wholly photographic (2.04)

Presentation (= dummy) Sample of a proposed publication, usually in the form of specimen pages. (Rates 2.10)

Print fee Not really a fee, but the cost of purchasing a copyprint from a picture source. Does not include reproduction fee. (3.11)

Print run The number of copies printed of a book or periodical. A print run may cover more than one edition.

Process engraving (= photo engraving) Obsolete term for the process whereby a picture is mechanically transferred to a relief block to make it suitable for letterpress printing. (4.07)

Promotion   Any form of activity designed to increase the sales or impact of a publication. (Rates 2.10)

Public domain, in the   Free of copyright. (2.12)

Publishers Association   (1.07)

Reference   The use of a picture as a guide to the artist, rather than for direct reproduction. Distinguish from ARTIST'S COPY. (Rates 2.10)

Relief printing   Printing processes in which the image is transferred from a block or plate from which everything except the image has been removed, leaving the image standing 'in relief' for transfer to the paper. (4.06)

Replacement fee   Paid to cover the cost of replacing a lost or spoiled picture. (3.10)

Reproduction fee   Paid for the right to reproduce an illustration. (2.10, 2.11)

Reproduction right   The right to reproduce an illustration. Distinguish from COPYRIGHT. (2.12)

Restrictions on use   (2.01)

Rotogravure   Photogravure when carried out on rotary machines for large-circulation periodicals. (4.07)

Royalty, pictures of   (2.04)

Screen   System of dots or pits created by putting a screen over an illustration to make it suitable for printing by the halftone or gravure processes. A picture so treated is said to 'have a screen'. (4.07, 4.08)

Search fee   Fee charged by a picture source to cover the cost of conducting research in its own files on a client's behalf. (2.10)

Service fee   Fee charged by a picture source to cover the costs incurred in servicing a client's request. (2.10)

Silk screen   Form of printing in which ink is forced through a fine mesh to form unbroken areas of tone. (4.07)

Slide   = Transparency, usually of 35mm size.

Space rates   Standard rates paid by a publication, generally newspapers and periodicals, for illustrations. Based on size. (2.10)

SPADEM   French organisation protecting copyright of member artists and their estates. (1.07)

SPREd   Society of Picture Researchers and Editors. British association for staff and freelance researchers. (1.07)

s/s   Same size.

Steel engraving   Form of print which, because it used hard steel, was able to achieve exceptional fineness. (4.06)

Stock photo   Photograph, not usually relating to matters of immediate current interest, held by picture sources—usually photo agencies—for possible use.

Syndication   The use of illustrations in publications additional to that for which they were originally procured, by agreement between the picture copyright holder and the client.

Transparency A colour photograph on transparent film, as opposed to a colour print on opaque material; resembles a negative, except that its colour values are positive. (4.08)

Voucher copy Copy of a book sent, before publication, free of charge to suppliers of illustrations to enable them to check the use made of their material. (3.12)

Woodcut, wood engraving Relief prints made (originally) from wood blocks, from which all except the required image has been cut away from the printing surface. (4.06)

World rights Sometimes the right to publish a book in any market in any language, but often more restricted. (3.11)

Xerox, xerography Form of photostat process. The word Xerox, a registered trade name, is often used of any kind of photostat, whatever the system. (3.08)

INDEX